Fun and Fancy
Machine Quiltmaking

Lois Tornquist Smith

American Quilter's Society
P.O. Box 3290
Paducah, KY 42001

Dedication

This book is dedicated to the twentieth century quiltmaker who values efficiency and creativity along with the time honored traditions of quiltmaking.

Many thanks to my students and friends for the encouragement and support given: Marjorie Coffey, Sue Pierce, Jill Ruspi, Janet and Steve Frye, Peter Ross, Gretchen Hill and Sharon Gilbert. Thank you Smith family, one and all, for the help given and for enabling me to devote my efforts toward this goal.

Additional copies of this book may be ordered from:

American Quilter's Society
P.O. Box 3290
Paducah, KY 42002-3290

@$19.95 Add $1.00 for postage and handling.

Copyright: Lois Tornquist Smith, 1989

This book or any part thereof may not be reproduced without the written consent of the Author and Publisher.

TABLE OF CONTENTS

Introduction

Part I: The Making Of A Quiltmaker

Part II: The Making Of A Quilt

Part III: The Making Of A Quilt Artist

BLOCK DESIGNS

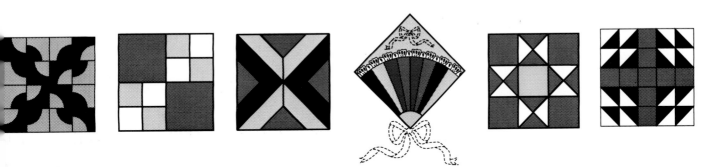

Prologue

Not every prospective quiltmaker has the opportunity to attend quiltmaking classes. This book is intended to be the "teacher by your side."

Part I is an introduction to the sewing machine and an overview of the quiltmaker. It assumes that the reader has little prior experience with either the sewing machine or quiltmaking. The basic machine instruction and vocabulary development are intended to quickly develop machine quiltmaking confidence and understanding.

The more experienced reader may use the introductory information as a refresher.

Part II presents detailed instruction for making a SAMPLER QUILT. The eight lessons simulate a teaching situation. Skills and techniques are illustrated for easy understanding. Designs and templates for quilt block patterns are given in ascending order of difficulty.

Though directions are given for making a SAMPLER QUILT, one block could be chosen and repeated to make an entire quilt.

Part III is included for the innovative craftsperson who enjoys unusual and out-of-the-ordinary techniques. Surface textures and other types of fabric manipulation are explored. The ideas detailed will more than likely trigger other surface design possibilities.

Quilts: A Place In Time

Something in the soul loves a quilt. TV advertising artists capitalize on this fact by furtively tucking quilts into the background of a two-second shot. Flashes of quilts on a rustic fence, hung on a wall or casually draped near the fireplace give the setting a feeling of love and devotion.

A few generations ago a young girl often started quilting at her grandmother's knee. Slowly she learned the art as she stitched, pulled out and replaced stitches that did not meet with adult approval. The childhood tears and anger were eventually replaced by pride as she developed her skills and her own standards. By the time she was 17, she had pieced a dozen tops all with increasing skill. Upon her engagement she made her finest quilt, her wedding quilt.

Time and circumstances changed the quiltmaking scene. Economic and social needs changed. It became more practical to buy a blanket for warmth than to make a quilt. "Quilting Bees" were no longer the main social event of the community now that homes and barns and churches were established.

Fewer quilts were made after the turn of the 20th century. Though the pace of quiltmaking slowed, it never became a lost art. The experience of piecing beauty from scrap had brought joy and hope to the pioneer and to the elite, and this sense of creation was kept alive.

The Bicentennial planners of 1976 sought to bring historical significance to the celebration by re-introducing some of the nearly lost arts and crafts of the previous two hundred years. Quiltmaking was just one of the revived crafts. What started as a quiet sharing of history turned into an explosion. Quiltmaking fever struck the heart of many. Manufacturers were alert and quickly responded by producing fabrics to encourage the new quiltmakers. New tools were suddenly available to speed the process.

There was a feeling of tenderness and excitement as the familiar old patterns were organized and compiled. Interest in quiltmaking began anew.

However, though the interest in quiltmaking was rekindled, there was no Grandma sitting in most corners with her scrap bag at her side. There was no one to say, "this is the way!"

Nevertheless, those who had put aside their quiltmaking skills started again to perfect their own abilities. Their stitches became smaller and more exact. They shared their knowledge with a new generation who was ready to learn. Many who were eager, however, had small children or were employed outside the home. While anxious to learn the skills of quiltmaking, they were in search of methods to meet their needs.

This book gently moves the art and joy of quiltmaking into a contemporary setting. The sewing machine combined with updated tools and techniques accelerates the quiltmaking process. Untouched is the heart and soul of quiltmaking which carries the message of love from one generation to the next stitched between the lines.

Lois Smith

Show & Tell

Beginning a quilt is easy. Like all quiltmaking, it involves a commitment of time and energy. The sewing machine, however, speeds every step along the way from the initial piecing to the final sashing and finishing.

The first part of this book features a SAMPLER quilt. Start big! Learn the fundamental techniques as you make a quilt. Once the basics are understood, there is freedom to explore new techniques and to deviate a bit from the traditional quiltmaking path.

There is little worry that your quilt project will be abandoned before it is finished. Machine quiltmaking is exciting! It is self-expression! It's fun!!!

Quiltmaking is the starting, finishing and sharing with pride the fruits of your labors of love.

In a classroom situation, "The Sampler" class is taught in eight sessions which meet every other week. At the last class meeting, a show date is scheduled. At the chosen time, students bring their quilt, friends, family and cameras for a celebration. These are wonderful occasions. Everyone is happy and proud.

PART ONE

The Making Of A Quiltmaker

Quiltmaking spans generations
with its product of love and
recorded history. Time modifies
the vocabulary and the tools,
but the heart of quiltmaking
remains constant.

Warming Up

The decision to make a quilt generally comes after several pleasant "quilt encounters." An inspiring quilt show may have stimulated your interest in quiltmaking. Maybe you have always had the desire deep in your heart to make a quilt. Suddenly you feel that the time is now.

The next thought that occurs is, "Can I make a quilt?"

Yes!! Of course you can!!

Many things in life demand a warm up or preparation. Quiltmaking is no exception.

☐ Acquaint yourself with the vocabulary and the terms associated with quiltmaking. That alone will help you gain confidence.

☐ Collect quilting tools before you begin your quilt. Once you have decided upon a project, it makes sense to have the right tools at hand from the outset. The rotary cutter, mat and ruler are probably the only tools you do not already have. Or you may have them tucked away in a bag in the closet waiting to be tried.

☐ Experiment with the rotary cutter. It will be your key to accuracy. Practice slicing up a piece of scrap fabric. Learning "rotary" will save you fabric and energy when you are making the quilt blocks.

☐ Play with your sewing machine. Some machines have been hiding in closets for years. Before you even think quilt color schemes, spend a little time with your machine getting acquainted with its parts and learning how to sew with that very important ¼" seam allowance.

☐ Establish yourself. See what you can do about claiming a little turf for you and your machine. I exchanged half of my laundry room for most of the basement for my "studio." It was well worth the trade-off.

The Basic Eighty . . .
A Quiltmaker's Vocabulary

Familiarity with these eighty words, and phrases and the items they describe, will
help make the quiltmaking instructions clear and easy to follow.

Alignment Pin – A pin dropped in the seamlines of joining pieces to perfectly position fabric intersection.

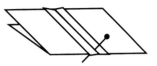

Applique – shapes sewn to a foundation fabric, thus creating a design.

Background – the receding or inconspicuous part of a block design.

Backing – fabric used for back side of quilt.

Back Stitching – reverse stitching often used at beginning and end of seam to secure stitches. Not generally used in machine piecing.

Batting – filler used in a quilt to give warmth and to add definition to the stitched designs.

Betweens – (needles) small, fine needles used in hand quilting.

(The) Betweens – (sashing) horizontal strips of fabric cut the width of a block and used to join blocks into vertical rows. (Horizontal Sashing.)

Block
Between
Block

Binding – narrow finishing strip on many quilts and wallhangings.

Blind Hem Stitch – a basic stitch found on most zig zag machines and used for invisible machine applique. ^ _ _ _ ^ _ _ _ ^ _ _ _ ^ _ _ _

Block – completed design unit, usually in the form of a square, which is sewn to other blocks to complete the quilt top.

Block-By-Block – construction techniques which enables a block to be pieced, sandwiched with batting and backing, and quilted before being assembled into the quilt.

Blocking Square – a grid drawn on an ironing board cover or fabric to facilitate accurate pressing.

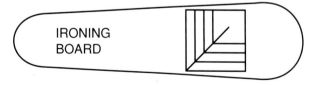

Borders – final or outside design rows of a quilt.

Chain Piecing – assembly line piecing of fabrics without cutting thread between units. A time and thread saver.

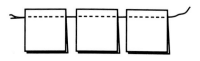

Cheater Cloth – printed fabric design that looks like a pieced or appliqued block.

Clean Finish – the straight or crisp fabric edge created when raw edge is trimmed away with rotary cutter.

Contemporary Blocks and Quilts – blocks designed today and quilts that are made today using traditional or contemporary patterns.

Color Wheel – a graphic arrangement of the color spectrum.

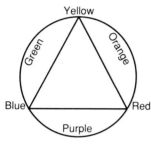

Core – the central blocks of a quilt sewn together before borders are added.

Corner Stones – small squares used at sashing intersections to add interest and to help align blocks.

Cutting Mat – a self-healing mat, preferably marked with a grid, used in conjunction with the rotary cutter and a sturdy ruler.

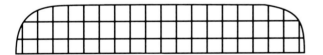

Decorative Stitches – machine stitches built into the machine or produced by cams and often used in machine quilting.

Disappearing Marking Pen – used for marking stitching lines on fabric. Line disappears by itself without water. (see also: marking pens.)

Double Stick Tape – transparent tape with two tacky surfaces. Used on bottom of plastic templates to secure the template to fabric for precise cutting.

Double Needle – two needles on one shaft used for pin tucking and sewing two rows of parallel stitching at one time.

Duckbill Scissors – sharp scissors with a duckbill-shaped blade. They are used for multi-layer cutting of straight and curved pieces as well as for close trimming of appliqued pieces.

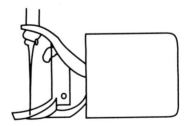

Elastic Thread – a stretchy thread which can be wound on the bobbin to create gathered or three-dimensional effects on fabric.

Even Feed Foot – special foot attachment which feeds the top and bottom layers of fabric evenly through machine. Also called a walking foot.

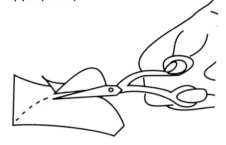

Feed Dogs – the cleats or pads which advance the fabric automatically through the machine as stitches are formed.

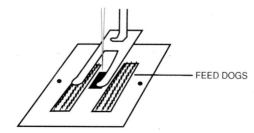

FEED DOGS

Feed Dogs Dropped – feed dogs inactivated either by dropping into the machine bed or covering with a plate to allow fabric to be moved manually for free motioning quilting.

Finished Size of Block – refers to size of block after it is sewn into a quilt. A 12″ block (finished size) block will measure 12½″ with seam allowance.

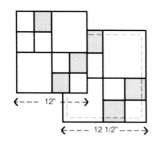

Fleece – A firm insulating fiber good for placemats, wallhangings, clothing and display boards.

Flexicurve – a flexible rubber bar used to draft curves and to mark sewing and cutting lines for curved patchwork.

Foundation – a block size piece of fabric used as the background for applique.

Free Motion Stitching – machine quilting done in a random but organized pattern with dropped feed dogs.

Freezer Paper – a grocery store product, used for pattern drafting, template making and as an aid in applique.

Grainline Awareness – thoughtful consideration given to the best possible grainline placement of pieces in a design.

Grainline – the direction of woven threads in a piece of fabric.
> **Bias** – a line diagonal to the grain in a fabric.
> **Cross Grain** – the alignment of fabric threads perpendicular to the selvage.

Lengthwise or Straight of Grain – the alignment of fabric threads parallel to selvage.

Selvage – the tightly woven finished edges of the fabric.

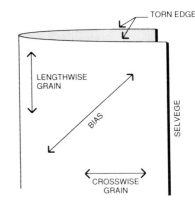

Marking Tools – pens or pencils used to place temporary marking lines on fabric:
> **Vanishing Pen** – writes with a purple line and disappears by itself within 24 hours or less depending upon the humidity.
> **Water Soluble Pen** – writes with a blue line and may be removed with cold water. Problems arise when ink is wicked into the batting causing the line to reappear.
> **Chalk** – comes in a variety of forms:
> • in a container with serrated dispensing wheel,
> • as a washout pencil in a variety of colors,
> • in a flat cake with sharp edge,
> • in a vanishing cake form.
> **Silver Pencil by Berol** – marks dark fabrics and is easily removed by gentle rubbing on scrap cloth.

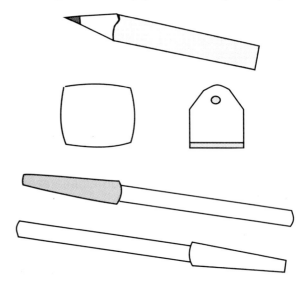

Meander Stitching – free motion stitching designs where lines generally do not cross one another.

Medallion – center design which is the main focus of a quilt. Borders surround center design and echo its design elements. This type of quilt is called a Medallion Quilt.

Miter – 45 degree angle seaming of border fabrics to form flowing quilt corners.

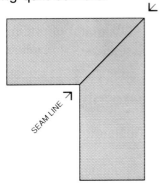

Pieced – a quilt or block made up of geometric shapes sewn together.

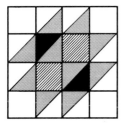

Points – sharp and complete ends of a pieced angle in a design. Star and triangle points should be complete and pointed, not blunted.

Point Turner – a blunt pointed tool for "poking out points" in applique.

Press – an up and down motion of the iron which produces a smooth surface but does not distort grainline. Ironing is a back and forth random movement of the iron.

(To) Quarter – to divide corresponding sides of border and quilt into fourths for accurate positioning and joining.

Quilt – two layers of fabric with an enclosed filler held together by stitching.

Quilting – the process of stitching the fabrics together.

Quilting Parts

FRONT

QUILT DEFINITIONS:

BLOCKS
BORDERS

CORNER STONES
SASHING

BACK

BACKING FABRIC

BACK OF BLOCKS
BACK OF SASHING

BACK OF BORDERS

15

Reference Point – marking on cut shapes to aid in proper alignment of pieces during piecing.

Regularly Patterned Fabric – yardage that is printed with a definite repeating design.

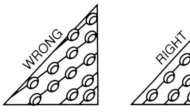

Rotary Cutter – cutting tool with a circular cutting blade for accurate and quick cutting of straight edges. The rotary cutter is also perfect for arthritic or handicapped hands.

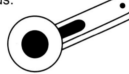

Sashing – the joining strips of fabric that surround and unify the blocks. Also called Stripping or Lattice.

    The Betweens – horizontal sashing strips.

    Vertical Sashing – the strips that run from the top to the bottom of quilt.

    Perimeter Sashing – outside rows of sashing enclosing quilt.

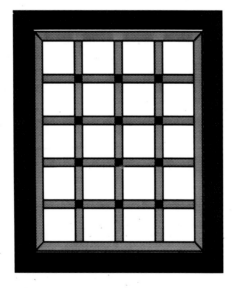

Scrap Quilt – a quilt made from many different fabrics, usually 50 or more. A scrap quilt can be made from new or collected fabrics.

Seam Ripper – small tool with sharp hooked end for removing stitches.

See Thru Ruler – sturdy plastic ruler used with rotary cutter.

Selvage – tightly woven edges of yardage. Should be removed and not be included in quilt piecing.

Shadow Through – distracting seam allowance lines which are visible due to improper pressing or use of fabric which is too thin or sheer. (Lining Required.)

Speed Piecing – techniques for assembly line piecing.

Stitching Spurs – short, unattractive lines of stitching on the back of the log cabin designs created by overstitching on the front of the log cabin.

Stitch-In-The-Ditch – stitching in the seamline.

Stripping – another name for Sashing.

Surface Texture – added stitching or manipulation of fabric to add dimension and interest to fabric.

Tagboard – lightweight cardboard sometimes used for templates.

Template – the pattern used for cutting design pieces.

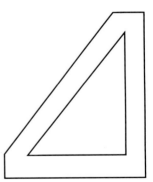

Template Plastic – clear or frosted plastic used to make templates.

Unit – the basic mathematical division of a quilt block. There are 4 basic units in a 4 Patch, 5 in a 5 Patch, etc.

Value – the lightness or darkness of a color.

Viewing Board – display board or area where work in progress can be hung to be viewed and evaluated.

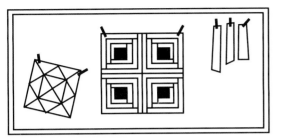

Walking Foot – same as Even Feed Foot.

Whiskers – short, clipped ends of thread that protrude from quilt surface when not properly trimmed or hidden.

Zinger – vibrant or unusual fabric which adds interest to quilt.

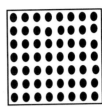

Tools And Equipment

Goal: Gather needed equipment so that your progress will not be hindered by the lack of the proper tool.

Organize the tools that you already have to eliminate searching for them.

Basic Equipment:
- ☐ A sewing machine (cleaned and oiled)
- ☐ A comfortable, adjustable sewing chair that allows you to look down upon your work in the machine
- ☐ Good lighting
- ☐ A handy ironing surface with grid for blocking
- ☐ A small iron
- ☐ A spray water bottle

Tools:
- ☐ Large-size rotary cutter (45mm diameter)
- ☐ Self-healing cutting board (18″ x 24″) or larger
- ☐ Long, heavy duty see-through plastic ruler (22″ or more)
- ☐ Quality 7″ scissors
- ☐ Duckbill scissors (optional but very helpful)
- ☐ Seam ripper

Notions:
- ☐ Long, glass headed quilting pins
- ☐ Magnetic pin holder
- ☐ Sewing thread (good quality cotton or polyester)
- ☐ Invisible nylon thread
- ☐ Vanishing fabric marking pen
- ☐ Chalk wheel
- ☐ Freezer paper
- ☐ 12″ vinyl floor tile
- ☐ Color wheel
- ☐ Flexicurve

Drafting and Template Equipment:
- ☐ Graph Paper (¼″ rule) Check for accuracy
- ☐ Pencil
- ☐ Pencil sharpener
- ☐ 12″ ruler
- ☐ Clear plastic sheets for template making
- ☐ Rubber cement
- ☐ Double stick tape
- ☐ Scissors for cutting paper or plastic
- ☐ Compass
- ☐ Yardstick compass

Organizing Tools:
- ☐ Notebook for organizing notes and storing templates
- ☐ Container for quilt fabrics
- ☐ Plastic bags for smaller scraps

Your Sewing Machine – Friend or Foe?

Quilts can be made on any well tuned sewing machine. Older machines may lack the blind hem stitch or zia-zag capability, but this deficiency can be overcome. A machine that runs smoothly and quietly while making secure, even stitches will be adequate for most quiltmaking. A cranky machine takes the fun out of sewing and should be taken to the repair shop for an over-haul. A positive working relationship with your sewing machine is important.

Understand and Care For Your Machine

Read the sewing machine manual that comes with your machine.

Learn where to oil your machine and tips for general maintenance.

Study the capabilities of your particular machine and learn to use them all.

Experiment with the various feet and interesting stitches. Keep them in mind as you progress, and use them as much as possible in new and innovative ways.

Brush out any lint caught under the feed dogs or around the shuttle. A hair dryer works well also to blow out little threads and dust. This brushing and cleaning should be repeated daily when working with polyester batting. Small fragments of the batting lodged in the machine can permanently etch and damage the hook which produces the stitch.

Oil reduces the friction on moving parts and keeps the machine running smoothly and quietly. If your machine looks over oiled, put a little alcohol on a lint free cloth and clean up the inside of the machine. Then oil machine with sewing machine oil before running the motor. Use a top grade oil recommended by your machine dealer. Oil moving parts after every eight hours of piecing or quilting.

Needles also need to be changed after every eight to ten hours of sewing, or sooner if they become burred or bent. Use a good quality needle. A medium sized needle, #11 or a #12/80 are the recommended size for piecing and most quilting.

Thread for piecing may be polyester, cotton or cotton/polyester. Thread should be high quality with long, staple fibers which give the thread a smooth appearance. Thread which is old and weak should be discarded.

Check your machine's performance:
- ☐ Verify threading and bobbin insertion with the owner's manual.
- ☐ Distance from needle to right side of presser foot should be ¼ inch. If not:
  - adjust needle position.
  - search accessories for ¼ inch presser foot.
  - purchase a ¼ inch presser foot.
- ☐ Thread machine with contrasting threads: one color in needle of machine, another color in bobbin.
- ☐ Sew two fabric scraps together to check tension:
  - needle thread *only* should show on top fabric.
  - bobbin thread *only* should show on bottom fabric.

If needle thread lies straight on the surface *pulling the bobbin thread up,* loosen *top* tension.

If the bobbin thread lies flat on the underneath surface, *pulling the needle thread down,* tighten *top* tension.

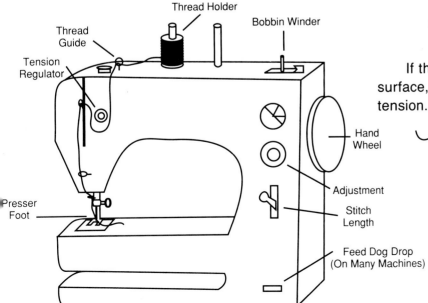

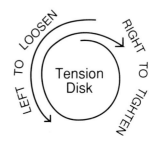

The Sewing Center – A Place For You!

Find yourself an area in which you can wallow in scraps and ideas without offending others in the household. An unused bedroom is ideal. A portion of the basement works well. You may have to settle for something less than ideal, but *organize* whatever area you choose. Refining your sewing room to meet your needs will be an on-going process. Be patient and creative.

Store unfinished projects along with the directions in a totebag or basket out of sight but within easy "finding distance."

File ideas for future use. Filing cabinets can help keep you organized and may also support your cutting table, if they are the proper height.

Clean up all possible clutter.

Hang up a viewing board where you can view work from a distance.

Save bags from fabric shopping trips. They recall happy memories and serve a good purpose. Tape them to your tables and sewing area to collect threads and scraps. This keeps the room neat and eliminates *de-threading* your finished work at a later date.

Work centers save time and frustration:

Cutting Center
  cutting board
  cutting wheel
  22″ ruler
  scissors
  double stick tape
  pencil

Viewing Board

Library: Arrange books
         alphabetically.

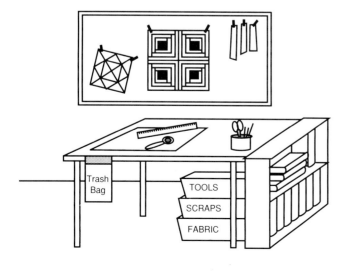

Sewing Center
  machine with accessories
  thread caddy nearby
  good lighting
  nippers or small scissors
  seam ripper
  6″ ruler

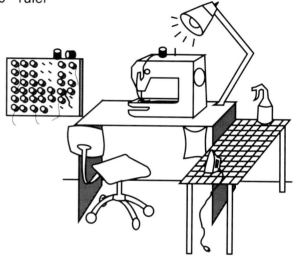

Pressing Area adjacent to sewing area
  small iron
  spray water bottle
  gridded blocking cloth

Storage Area

Drafting Area
  You may not have a separate area exclusively reserved for drafting. However, *keep all drafting equipment together*:
    graph paper
    pencils
    pencil sharpener
    ruler
    template plastic
    rubber cement
    paper scissors
    compass
    yard stick compass
    flexicurve

In addition to the necessities, add, if possible, the things that will make the sewing even more enjoyable: a telephone and a radio or stereo system.

The Rotary Cutter

The *rotary cutter* is a tool fairly new to quiltmaking. It has proven to be a most efficient tool which is easy to use and which produces excellent results for straight line cutting without marking fabric.

The rotary cutter is used in conjunction with a semihard surfaced *mat* and sturdy clear ruler which is at least 22" long, or the width of a piece of folded fabric. A ruler that has a plainly marked ¼" marking along one long side and a ½" marking along the other is helpful.

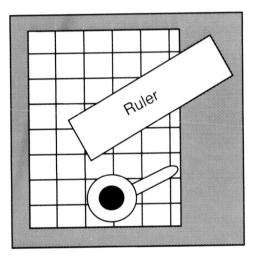

One excellent ruler that is available has a lip on one short side which fits over the side of the cutting board acting as a T-square while helping to *stabilize* the ruler during cutting.

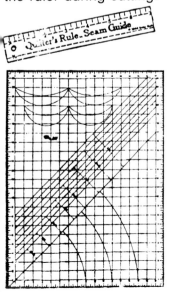

A short *sturdy* 6" clear ruler is an asset. The ruler is placed over the template and protects the template edge during cutting.

The mat must be made of self-healing composition that will not be shredded by the sharp blade nor should it be so rigid that it dulls the rotary blade. The mat which is marked with precise 1" grid marking is suggested for cutting strips of fabric as well as for trimming up the blocks after they are quilted.

(Some directions suggest cutting on the plain side of the mat instead of the side with the grid. I disregard their advice to have the advantage of using the grid for more accurate cutting. It doesn't seem to harm the mat.)

Rotary Cutter Method

The rotary cutter looks and performs like a pizza cutter. By rolling the cutter along the ruler's edge two or more layers of folded fabric will be precisely cut into strips which will then be cut into smaller pieces for seaming.

For a *right handed* person, the aligned raw edges of the fabric will be coming from the right side to the left, the fold of the fabric will be nearest your body.

A *left handed* person will work with the fabric coming from the left hand side, fold closest to your body.

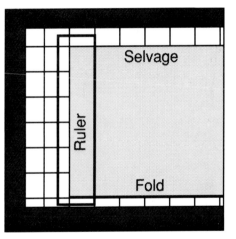

Trim the torn edges of the fabric by covering the raw edges with the ruler and trimming off ¼". This is called *clean finishing* the edge.

☐ Position the flat side of the wheel against the ruler.
☐ Use downward pressure on the wheel.
☐ Move the cutter along ruler away from your body.

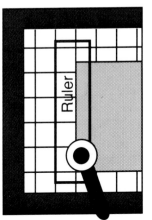

PART TWO

The Making Of A Quilt

The Sampler Quilt

Frye SAMPLER by Janet Frye.

The SAMPLER QUILT incorporates many quiltmaking techniques into one quilt, making it a natural place to start machine quiltmaking.

Part Two of this book will be divided into eight lessons. Each lesson is similar to a classroom teaching session. The material covered can realistically be completed in a two week time period.

Suggestions and patterns are given for making 12″ blocks. The quilt blocks will be *pieced, appliqued* or *string quilted*. Log Cabin and Crazy Patch blocks will be made also. The progression is chosen to increase skill level from one block to the next. Each new block presents a slightly different challenge in color choices as well as in technique.

Block-by-block construction will be used in making the SAMPLER. After a block design has been completed, the block will be layered with batting and backing and machine quilted. Since the block "package" is only about 12 inches square, you will have maximum freedom to machine quilt without bulk.

When all the blocks have been quilted individually, they will be sewn together with a unifying sashing to complete the quilt. This type of construction works well. There is never a lot of bulk to squeeze through the machine.

A SAMPLER is unique in that it does *not* take a lot of *preplanning*. There is no need to draw a specific design layout. You can jump in with both feet and get started. The final arranging of the blocks is done after the blocks have been completed to assure a pleasant balance of color design.

Gathering Fabrics

The quilt begins and gets its impact from the fabrics and their colors. This is an exciting part of the quiltmaking process.

Selecting Fabrics

A SAMPLER QUILT can accommodate a wide variety of fabrics. Depth and interest come from having a good color scheme well executed. While you are learning the fundamentals of machine quiltmaking, you are also having fun placing fabrics next to one another and discovering relationships of color and value.

Manufacturers of quilt fabrics are aware that many quilters feel inadequate when it comes to selecting fabrics for a quilt. Therefore, they have consulted with quilt artists and researched the quilt fabrics from the past to create lines of fabric which are pleasing and workable in both color and design. Each line includes a variety of prints and solids in several different color runs.

These lines of fabrics are intended to aid the quiltmaker in making a beautifully coordinated quilt. The scale of prints is varied and the colors blend well. *Exclusive* use of a line of fabrics should be resisted, however, to avoid a "mass produced" and unimaginative appearance. Other fabrics should be included to personalize the quilt and give it a uniqueness.

Fabric stores specializing in quiltmaking are the best place to shop for coordinating quilt fabrics. Quilt shops have high quality fabrics and knowledgeable salespeople.

Choose A Key Fabric

If possible, start your fabric selection with a multi-colored, interesting stripe, similar to striped wall paper.

Think of this fabric as your *key fabric*, the one that will set the stage for your quilt.

This type of stripe will add special interest to the body of the quilt when cut up into geometric shapes. It can be used again to border the quilt. This one fabric alone can unify the entire quilt, as well as being the coordinator for the remaining fabric selections.

If your are unable to settle on a stripe, find a multi-colored print. It will serve the same purpose.

Visualize The Effect You Want

Before choosing the other fabrics, *visualize* a quilt built around this particular fabric. Take another step and *relate* your "quilt" to something in your experience! Does it give the feel of *Mardi Gras* or *The Fourth of July*? Do the soft pastels make you think of ice cream sherbet? By studying the key fabric and identifying its characteristics, you will be better able to select fabrics to build the quilt you envision.

Does the *key fabric* bring to mind a *season*?
- ☐ Spring – fresh greens, new birth, flowers, the artist Monet
- ☐ Summer – bright, bold, clear, warm colors, fireworks, VanGogh
- ☐ Winter – white, cold, frosted, the paintings of Andrew Weyth
- ☐ Fall – rich earth tones, golds, rusts, Rembrandt

Do you recognize a special *mood* or *feeling* from this fabric?
- ☐ Country – soft, muted, small prints, plaids
- ☐ Traditional – muted fabrics, large and small prints
- ☐ Dramatic – bold, bright prints, sharp contrasts
- ☐ Juvenile – bright, bold, primary colors, happy
- ☐ Patriotic – red, white, blue, flags, stars, stripes
- ☐ Holiday – red and green, orange and black

Hang on to your mental picture and select fabrics to produce that image.

Choose Fabrics Carefully

Select fabrics in a wide variety of prints (small to large scale) and color values (light to dark). Fabrics do not have to match each other, but all fabrics should blend or relate to the key fabric.

A 20 block quilt (twin or double bed) will require a minimum of *seven yards* assorted *100% cotton* for the quilt block designs. Additional fabrics will be needed for the back, sashing and borders, but that will be selected later. (Please see *Fabric Requirement* chart.)

Fabrics
Required For Quilt Block Designs

Twin	20 Blocks	7½ yards assorted fabrics
Double/Queen	20 Blocks	7½ yards assorted fabrics
King	25 Blocks	8½ yards assorted fabrics

Select

☐ One yard of the *key fabric*, stripe or multi-colored.

Purchase 3½ yards more if you plan to use this fabric in a border also.

☐ *Prints* which coordinate with the stripe or key fabric.
   A. *Small* over-all print (½ yard)
   B. *Medium*-sized print (½ yard)
   C. *Large* wide-spaced print (½ yard)
   D. *Large* over-all floral (½ yard)

☐ *Prints* with different color values:
   A. *Light* colored fabric (½ yard)
   B. *Medium* colored fabric (½ yard)
   C. *Dark* colored fabric (½ yard)
   D. *Extra Dark* colored fabric (½ yard)

☐ One or two solid fabrics (½ yard of each).

☐ Small over all light print for background (1 yard).

(For variety and interest, select two fairly similar fabrics and get ¾ yard of each.)

☐ Zippy fabric for accent (¼ yard).

Buy a self-limiting quarter of a yard to avoid the possibility of oveuse. (See page 131 for complete yardages.)

Stack Bolts and Step Back!!

Before purchasing your fabrics, stack the bolts of fabrics, graduating the color values from light to dark.

Take a good look at the combined fabrics. If there are big gaps, fill them in with other fabrics. You are looking for a gradual blending from light to dark that is personally pleasing. Look for a smooth flow of color and value, not waterfalls and rapids.

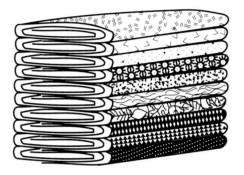

Have Yardages Cut.

Backing

The backing fabric (see *backing totals, page 131*) should coordinate with the top fabrics. An overall print works very well. Stripes and plaids should be avoided since the back will be cut into block size working sections and matching the design lines would be a problem.

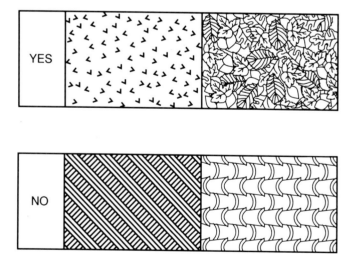

While *solid fabrics* do not present design problems, any quilting flaws will be visible and shading variations due to grainline position of the block in quilt are obvious.

Batting

Regular loft glazed polyester works the best for a quilt that is to be machine quilted block by block. It seems to grab the fabric and not slide around during the quilting process. The regular loft allows for quilting with definition without pucker.

Machine quilting has a tendency to compress a block somewhat. *Low loft batting* which is initially very thin results in a quilt that is very flat.

High loft batting is recommended for baby quilts or comforters which are to be tied; not recommended for machine quilting.

Fleece is a more solid filler and is usable but does not give the quilting dimension found in the regular loft batting.

Sashing or Stripping

Front sashing fabric will be selected after blocks have been completed. (see Lesson 7.)

Borders will also be finalized at the completion of the blocks and the quilt core. However, if a stripe has already been purchased to use within the quilt blocks and is also planned for the border, it should be purchased while it is still available. (see page 131.)

Wash Fabrics

Wash fabrics in *warm soapy water*. Divide fabrics into lights and darks. Wash separately to remove excess dye. Reds and very dark fabrics should be washed at least twice or until no more dye is released. Dry in the dryer. Fabrics may shrink about 1″ per yard. Press with an iron or smooth with your hand.

The batting does not need to be washed.

Bleeding Fabrics

1 cup of white vinegar per gallon of water will set some bleeding fabrics. If fabric still does not appear to be set, do not use the material in a quilt.

Helpful Hint: Keep a *Fabric Swatch Record*
☐ Snip a small piece from each fabric selected.
☐ Slip these onto a safety pin or glue to a small card to carry in your purse.
☐ Make a *Fabric Swatch Record* for your notebook also.
☐ Noting where you purchased fabric may prove helpful.

Lesson One - Four Patch Designs

Making Templates
Cutting and Grainline Techniques
Cutting from Stripes

Block Organization: Color and Design
Piecing
Piecing: Standards of Good Workmanship

Pressing
4 Patch Blocks and Suggestions
Templates

''Yard by yard, life is hard; inch by inch it's a cinch.''

There are many skills to be considered and learned in the process of making a quilt. By working step by step through the following chapters you will soon feel confident and accomplished.

The Four Patch designs are the first quilt blocks to be constructed in your quilt. Start with an easy design and do it well.

Goal:
Learn to recognize four patch blocks
Make five different four patch blocks

Skills:
Template Making
Cutting Techniques
Piecing Techniques
Block Construction

Four Patch

Design Categories

Before a design can be recreated in fabric, the organization of the block design has to be recognized.

In this block, the Double Four Patch, a close look will reveal 4 equally-sized sections. All 4 sections of the block are the same size even though two sections are made up of only *one piece* while the remaining sections each have 4 *smaller pieces*. This is a *four patch block*.

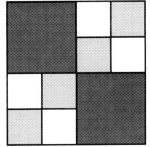

When the block category is determined, the block can be divided into units. The 12″ 4 patch design has a basic unit of 6″. Each 6″ unit will be subdivided into different shapes.

To make a quilt block, these shapes are made into patterns or *templates*.

Templates

Templates will be made of durable *plastic* and are *reusable*.

Each 6″ unit block will be subdivided into shapes.

Shapes will be isolated and ¼″ seam allowance will be added to each.

An unlimited number of designs can be made by combining these resulting geometric shapes.

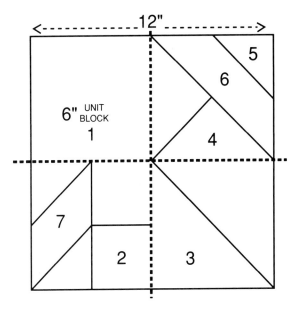

Making Template

Accurate patterns are included with each section of this book. You may carefully trace these patterns onto graph paper, glue to template plastic with rubber cement and cut out with paper scissors. *Label* each template so that it may be reused. Include the following: 12″ block; 4 patch; date; your initials.

Templates are the foundation of a quilt that is square and true. Templates must be made very accurately.

You may choose to draft your own templates to extend your quiltmaking knowledge and flexibility. Once you learn to make your own templates, you will be able to draft almost any design in any size block.

Templates required to make suggested 4 Patch Blocks:

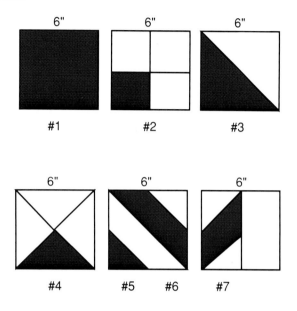

Graph Paper Method of Template Drafting

☐ Draw basic unit block on graph paper.
☐ Divide as indicated in the above diagram.
☐ Add ¼″ seam allowance on all sides of desired shape.
☐ Cut out and glue to plastic with rubber cement.
☐ Cut out template precisely.
☐ Mark grainline.
☐ Label: 12″ block; 4 patch; date

To Draft 6″ Unit Square

☐ Draw a 6″ square on graph paper.
☐ Add ¼″ seam allowance.
☐ Cut out square beyond seam allowance.
☐ Glue graph paper to template plastic with rubber cement.
☐ Carefully cut on seam allowance line.
☐ Label template:
   • size of block – 12″ Block
   • design classification – 4 Patch
   • grainline preference
   • your initials and date

To Make Triangle Template

☐ Draw a 6″ square.
☐ Divide into triangles.
☐ Add seam allowance to one triangle only.
☐ *Blunt* the extending points of the triangle, leaving ¼″ seam allowance.

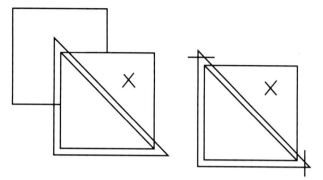

Note: Graph paper markings cannot be used to ad[d] ¼″ seam allowance to diagonal sides. Use the ¼ on see-through ruler.

To make the remaining templates:
☐ Draw the basic 6″ Unit block.
☐ Divide block as indicated.
☐ Add seam allowance on all sides.
☐ Cement to plastic.

Cutting and Grainline

Careful attention to cutting is critical to a wel[l] executed block. If the pieces are cut off grain or il[l] sized, they will always remain that way. Good cuttin[g] techniques pay dividends.

Grainline refers to the direction of the wove[n] thread in a piece of fabric. The *lengthwise* or *straigh[t] of grain* runs parallel to the selvage and is th[e] strongest and the straightest grainline.

The *Horizontal Grainline* is called the *Cross Grain*. That too is fairly stable and straight even though it ma[y] not be exactly perpendicular to the selvage and it doe[s] have a small amount of stretch.

Bias edges (- - - - - -) are weak and stretchy. *Avoid* the use of *bias* on the outside edges of a block when possible and practical because the edge of the block will ripple.

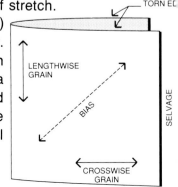

Theoretically, if nothing else were to be considered, all the grainlines in a block would be placed to run in a specific direction. The straight of grain would always run "north and south," the cross grain would always run "east to west."

The preferred grainline is marked on each template with an arrow. This *direction line* should be placed on the fabric to follow the lengthwise grainline.

The Golden Rule of Grainline

Whenever possible and practical . . .

avoid the use of bias grainline
on the outside edges of a block.

Creative Grainline Cutting

A straight edge will *stabilize* a bias seam.

When two long bias seams are to be sewn together, it may be attractive and desirable to cut the longest piece straight of grain.

(See *Wheels and Windblown Square*, page 34.)

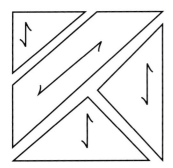

Stripes should be cut to add *design interest* to a block, regardless of grainline.

(See *Jacob's Ladder,* page 43; *Card Trick*, page 44.

Prints should be cut so they are *visually pleasing* even if it means they will be cut slightly "off grain."

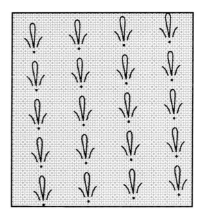

Cutting takes care, common sense, creativity and a grainline awareness.

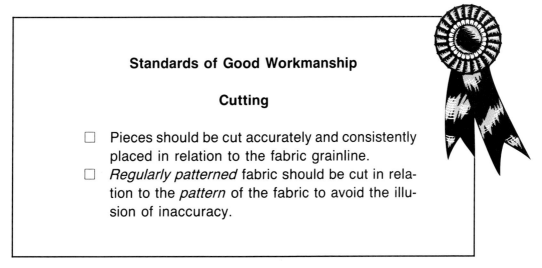

Standards of Good Workmanship

Cutting

☐ Pieces should be cut accurately and consistently placed in relation to the fabric grainline.

☐ *Regularly patterned* fabric should be cut in relation to the *pattern* of the fabric to avoid the illusion of inaccuracy.

Pieces From Strips

Using the *rotary cutter* to *cut* geometric shapes from a *cut strip* of fabric produces excellent results.

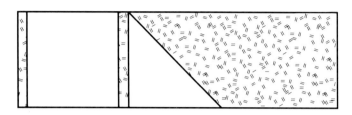

- ☐ Cut fabric strip the depth of *unit template* times fabric width.
- ☐ Cut one strip from each of your fabrics.
- ☐ Use fabric strips for cutting geometric shapes.
  - • Place double stick tape on bottom of template.
  - • Place taped side of template on fabric.
  - • Protect template with sturdy short ruler.
  - • Cut around template and ruler with rotary cutter.

Strip Advantages:
- ☐ Working with small piece of fabric is comfortable.
- ☐ Results are accurate.
- ☐ Color Combinations are easier to visualize with small fabric pieces.
- ☐ Several layers can be cut simultaneously.
- ☐ Room clutter is reduced.
- ☐ In the long run, less fabric will be wasted.

Stripes, plaids and *regularly patterned fabrics* should be cut *individually* to assure precise alignment of pattern and template.

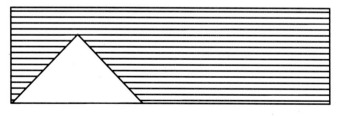

Position template carefully, *centering* on *design* of fabric.

Alternate Multilayer Cutting Method

Sometimes you may not be in a position to use the rotary cutter. Sharp scissors will cut many layers accurately also. The *duckbill* scissors with their short sharp blades do an exceptional job of cutting without having any shifting in the fabrics.
- ☐ *Layer* or fold fabrics.
- ☐ *Iron layers* to hold fabrics together.
- ☐ *Position template* on fabric.
- ☐ *Draw* around template with pencil.
- ☐ *Cut on* pencil line. *Using duckbill or regular sharp scissors.*

Color and Design

Fabric Choices

One of the fascinations of quiltmaking is the joy of working with *color* and *design*. The planning of a block involves putting one fabric with another. *Colors* must be placed to look attractive and to present the *design* of the block to its best advantage.

A quilt block is most often composed of two elements: *A design* and a *background*. The design is meant to capture the attention of the viewer. The *background* is meant to be low key and not fighting for attention. A *contrast* between design and background is vital to the success of a design.

Piecing is the sewing together of the design pieces. If it is neat and accurate, it adds strength and clarity to the design. When the seamlines are misaligned, the design becomes confused and unattractive.

The fabrics selected at the store are your *palette*. They will make the designs sing and dance. As you

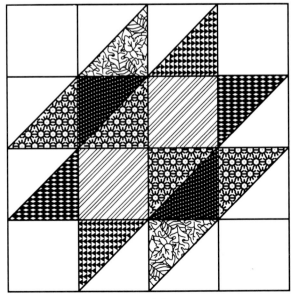

Anvil

"play" with your pieces, you may find a fabric that doesn't work. Don't use it if you don't like what is does in your quilt.

It is always fun to add a few pieces as you work along. Trade fabrics with your friends, dig into your collected fabrics to see what you might add to your quilt palette. You are not limited to your original seven yards.

When adding new pieces to your originally selected group of fabrics, make sure that they too blend with the *key fabric*. If you find a particular color that works well, try to find another fabric that is similar in color but different in pattern scale.

- [ ] *Select block pattern* to be pieced.
- [ ] Determine *design* areas and *background* or neutral areas.
- [ ] *Choose fabrics* for piecing the design using a variety of light, medium and dark color values in a variety of print sizes.

Between Cutting and Sewing

As the pieces are cut, they should immediately be placed *in design position*. A piece of polyester fleece works well for this.

Positioning Fleece

Polyester fleece is a sturdy lofted fabric that is excellent for temporarily positioning cut design pieces.

The fleece has almost a "magnetic" attraction which holds the piece securely until needed. The design can even be hung on a wall for viewing from a different angle.

A 15" x 15" square will allow plenty of room for laying out a design.

Have several squares cut and handy. Some days *creative color designs* just seem to flow. Use this time to cut several blocks and position them on the fleece for piecing later.

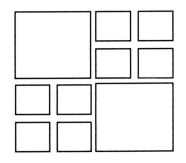

Fabric choices should be evaluated.

Is this what you had in mind? Do you suddenly have a better idea? Don't be afraid to make substitutions and *recut* a piece or two. I have been known to recut practically the whole block until I have gotten the feeling that I wanted in the design.

Save any unused pieces. Chances are that they will get a second chance to be used before the quilt is finished.

Machine Piecing

Piecing is the sewing together of small pieces to make *units*. The units are generally sewn into *rows*, the rows are sewn into the finished *block*.

To *join* pieces together:
- [ ] Place right sides of fabric facing each other, "right sides together."
- [ ] *Sew* with a ¼" seam allowance.

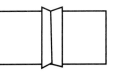

- [ ] 16 stitches per inch.

- [ ] Stitch from edge of fabric to opposite edge.

- [ ] Do not *backstitch*.
- [ ] *Press* seams *open*.

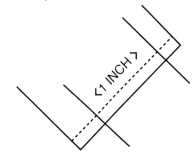

Machine stitched seams are very strong and are not weakened by being *pressed open*.

An open seam presents less bulk when being joined to "like pieces" and makes the intersecting seam line easier to align.

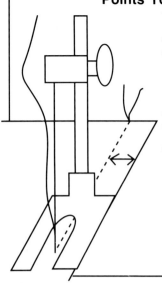

Points To Remember

The distance from the *needle* to the right side of the *presser foot* **must** be ¼".

Backstitching is intended to lock beginning and ending stitching. When piecing with 16 stitches per inch, the *tight stitch* prevents stitches from pulling out. *Backstitching* is therefore unnecessary.

Intersections require careful matching:
- ☐ Place units right sides together.
- ☐ *Match stitching lines.*
- ☐ Drop *"Alignment"* pin through *stitching lines.*
- ☐ Check opposite side to see that pin is in seam line.
- ☐ *Reposition* alignment pin, if necessary.
- ☐ Fasten pin in fabric.
- ☐ Add *security pins* on both sides of *alignment pin.*
- ☐ Sew seam, *removing pins* as you sew.
- ☐ *Press* seams *open.*

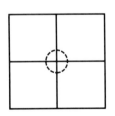

Standards of Good Workmanship

Piecing

- ☐ *Points* on triangles and stars should be *complete.*
- ☐ *Intersections* should be precisely matched.
- ☐ Pieces should *fit together* and *lay flat.*
- ☐ *Thread* color should not show in the seams.
- ☐ Seams should not *shadow through.*
- ☐ *Seams* should be strong and apparently long-lasting.
- ☐ *Pressing* should not *distort* block.

Step By Step – The Double Four Patch

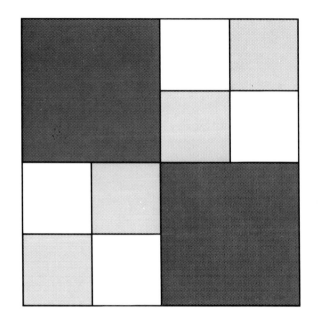

- ☐ *Select* appropriate *templates*:
  Use templates #1 and #2. (Learn to see the templates as fractions of the *unit square.*)
- ☐ *Choose the Fabrics*:
  Blocks require a pleasing *variety* in value (light and dark) and in print size and spacing.

Remember this ditty every time you select fabrics for a block:

Light, Medium, Dark: (values)
Small, Medium, Large: (prints)

- ☐ Layout total block.
- ☐ Join smallest pieces first.
- ☐ Press seams open.
- ☐ Sew into units, matching seam lines.
- ☐ Press seams open.
- ☐ Join units into rows.
- ☐ Join rows into block.
- ☐ Make intersection seams match perfectly.
- ☐ Press carefully again.
- ☐ Measure block. It should be 12½". (12" plus two ¼" seam allowances.)

It only takes a little more effort to do it right!!!
Your seam ripper is your friend!

Remember Basic Block Construction

☐ *Join* smallest pieces first.

☐ *Press seams open.*

☐ *Sew* into *units.*

☐ *Join* units into *rows.*

☐ *Join* rows into *block.*

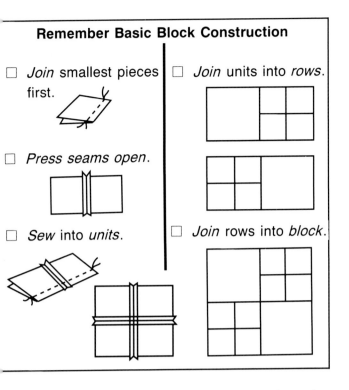

When a block has been finished, hang it on the *viewing board* or on a wall. Seeing the fabric combinations from a distance gives a new perspective. Each completed block will help make future fabric choices. *Continue* with a successful color combination, make *substitution* in pattern or in color. *Learn* from *your experience.*

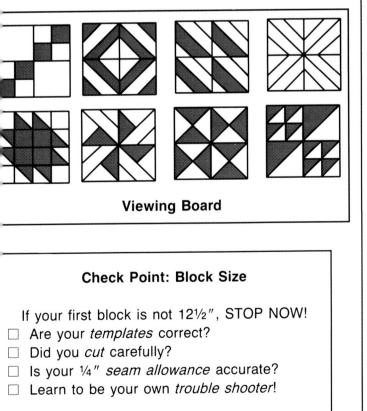

Viewing Board

Check Point: Block Size

If your first block is not 12½", STOP NOW!
☐ Are your *templates* correct?
☐ Did you *cut* carefully?
☐ Is your ¼" *seam allowance* accurate?
☐ Learn to be your own *trouble shooter*!

Understand the *Standard of Good Workmanship*, but set your own goals! Every quiltmaker has times when points get blunted or something is less than perfect. Quiltmaking should be fun! Always work to perfect your skills, but don't let perfection spoil your quiltmaking enjoyment!!

Pressing

The importance of pressing cannot be overstressed. Every seam must be pressed open before it is crossed over with another seam. The total block must be carefully pressed before it can be placed on the batting and quilted. Pressing is an integral part of a successful quilt.

The closer the iron and ironing pad are to your sewing machine, the more likely you will be to do a good job of pressing.

Pressing: Key To Success

Small pieces can either be *distorted* or *worked into shape* with the iron. *Establish* good techniques.

☐ Draw a right angle *blocking square* on ironing board or separate fabric using permanent ink. *Or*
☐ *Buy* a gridded ironing board cover.
☐ *Press* after aligning edges of pieced section with grid lines of blocking square.
☐ *Mist* with spray water bottle.
☐ *Press* again until dry.

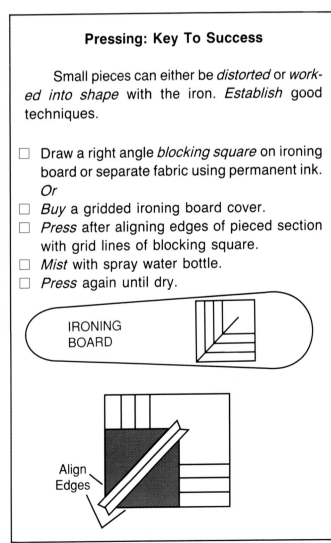

Four Patch Blocks

Flock of Geese

This block is always an eye catcher whether done in scrap fabrics or two strikingly different fabrics.

Choose fabrics that contrast well with one another to achieve the push-pull effect of equally balanced light and dark areas.

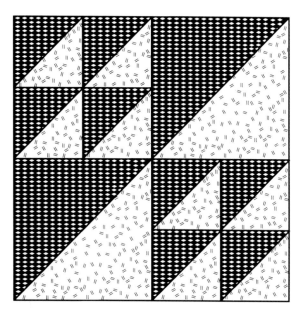

Chain piece triangles together by feeding them through the machine without cutting the thread between the sets of pieces.

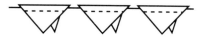

The joining edge of the triangles is cut "on the bias." Take care in sewing and pressing to avoid distortion.

Yankee Puzzle

- [ ] *One template* is used to construct this design.
- [ ] Use two or more fabrics.
- [ ] Place *long edge* of template on straight of grain to avoid bias outer edges.

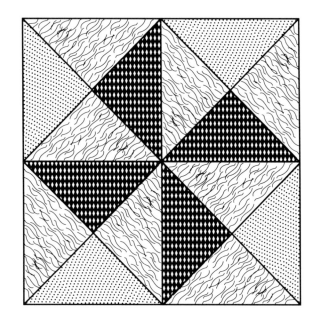

Check Point: Size Comparison

A pieced unit should be equal in size to the *unit template*.

These 3 designs can be made with the same 2 templates. Each *unit square* is pieced identically.

A more pleasing visual affect may be achieved by placing the long side of the *trapezoid* template (#6) on the *straight of grain*. Care should be taken to not stretch the resulting *bias outside edge*.

Lightning

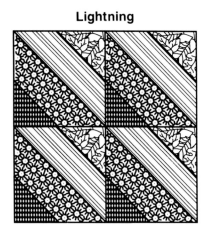

Kings X

God's Eye

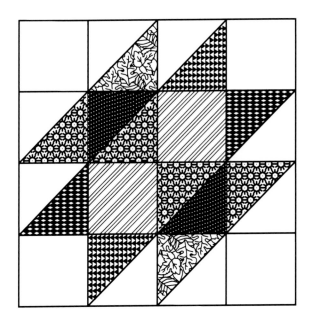

The Anvil

- [ ] *A scrap block* adds interest and integrates fabrics.
- [ ] Keep *Anvil* color values similar to hold design together.
- [ ] After laying out design, sew pieces together *a set at a time* rather than chain piecing to avoid confusion in placement.

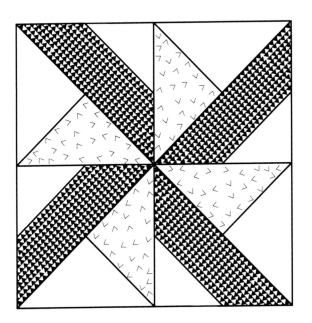

Wheels

- [ ] Block gives feeling of movement.
- [ ] Long side of *Trapezoid* (#6) may be cut *with* the straight of grain to add *visual strength* to the block. This will also stabilize bias edges of triangles.
- [ ] *Trapezoid* in this block is *not* reversible. *Cut 4 identical shapes.*

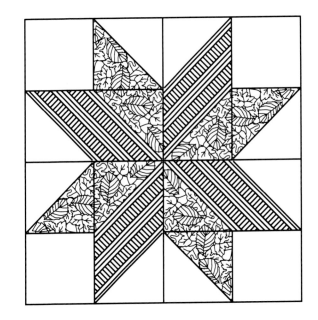

Star Flower

- [ ] Stars add crispness to a quilt when well done.
- [ ] All star points can be made by joining two small triangles *or* alternate *star points* can be cut from stripe using *parallelogram* template. Cut 4 *identical* stripe points. Pattern is *not* reversible in this block.
- [ ] Lay out design. Piece in *rectangles* rather than in rows.

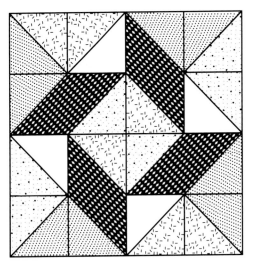

Windblown Square

- [ ] Block shows rhythm and depth.
- [ ] Combine two *very similar* background fabrics for added interest.
- [ ] *Piece* block in *rectangles*.
- [ ] *Parallelogram* is not reversible. *Cut 4 identical parallelogram* design pieces.

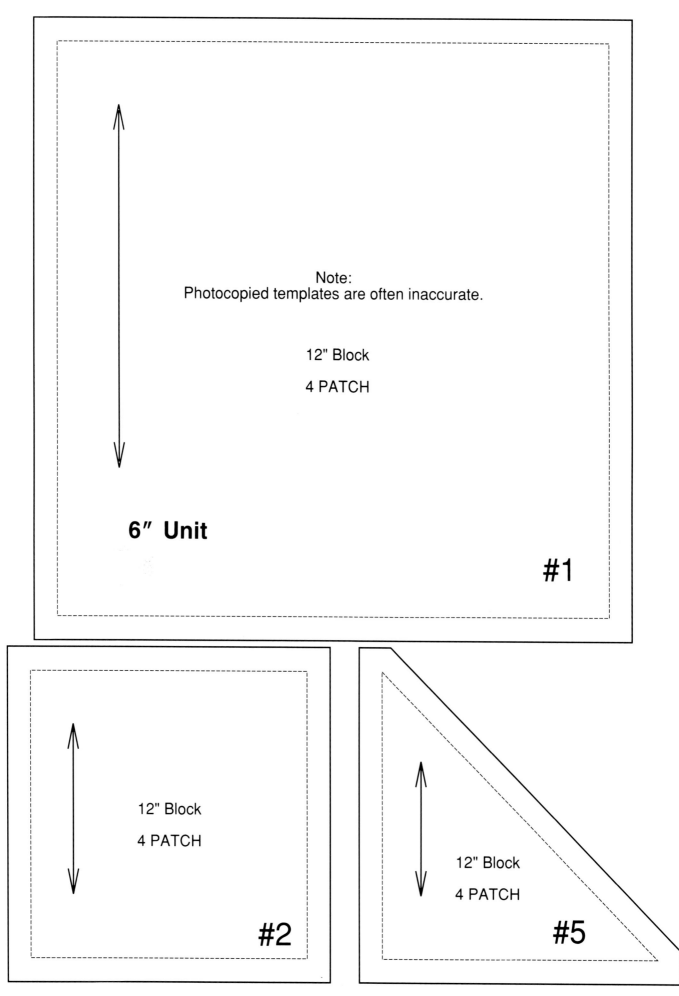

Note:
Photocopied templates are often inaccurate.

12" Block

4 PATCH

6" Unit

#1

12" Block

4 PATCH

#2

12" Block

4 PATCH

#5

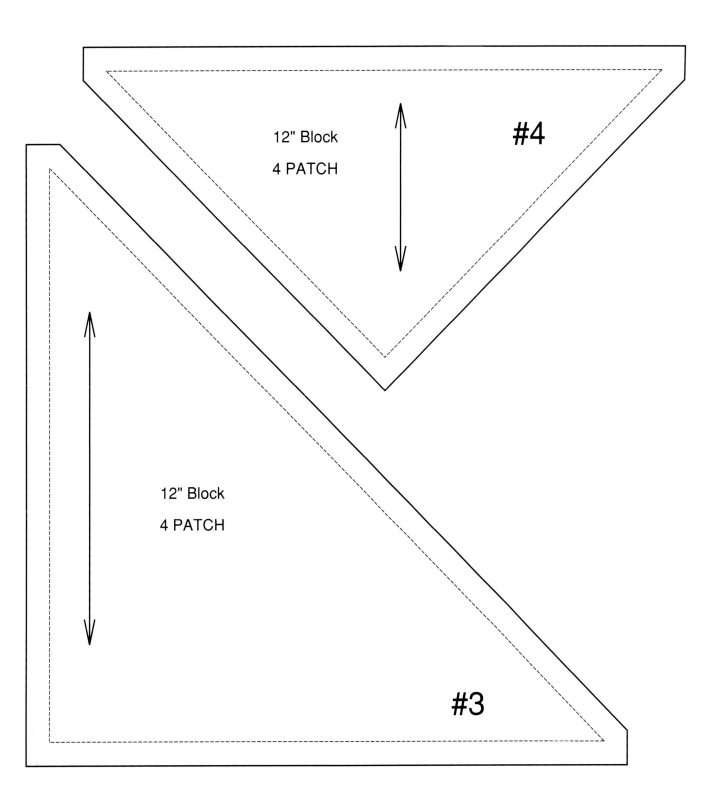

12" Block
4 PATCH

#4

12" Block
4 PATCH

#3

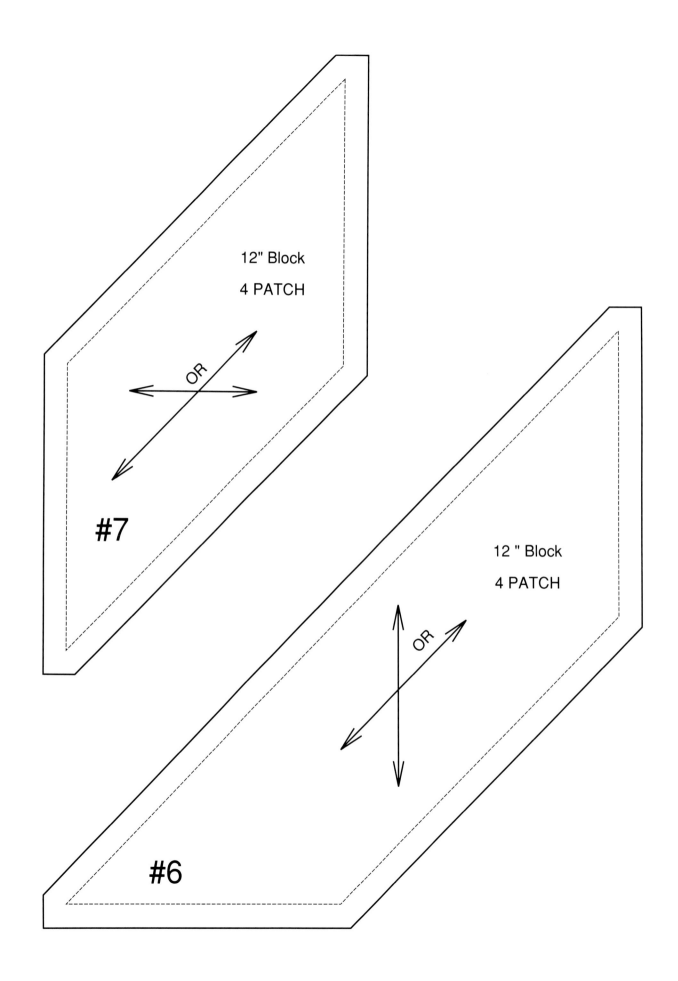

12" Block

4 PATCH

OR

#7

12 " Block

4 PATCH

OR

#6

Lesson Two - Nine Patch Designs

Template Construction
9 Patch Blocks and Suggestions
Speed Piecing

Decorative Stripes
Creative Color Placement
Quilt Backing

Quilt Backing: Standards of Workmanship
Quilt Batting
9 Patch Templates

Share your quiltmaking with a friend, and watch the excitement and anticipation spread!

In a teaching situation, the first part of every class is devoted to *Show and Tell*. Finished blocks are shown and admired. Small problems are discussed and solved. This wonderful sharing is the heart and soul of quiltmaking. See if you can find a quilting buddy.

Goal:
   Select and *piece* five 9 Patch Blocks

Skills:
   Speed piecing
   Working with stripes

   Backing squares
   Quilt sandwich

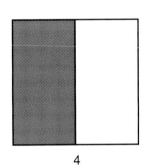

1

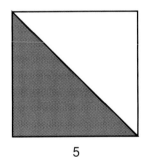

3

2

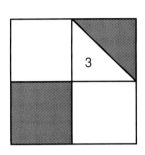

4

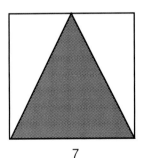

5

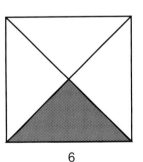

6

7

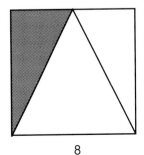

8

The Nine Patch Blocks are similar to the Four Patch Blocks. The division of the block is changed. The Nine Patch Block has three divisions across the top of a 12″ square. The Unit Block will be a 4″ square plus seam allowance.

Templates for the Nine Patch Blocks are given in the book. If you *draft* your own templates, *use the 4″ basic unit*.

Make all eight 9 Patch templates.
Label: 12″ Block, 9 Patch, Date, initials.

Album

- ☐ Center could be used as *signature* area or for creative piecing or quilting.
- ☐ This block offers a wide range of possibilities depending on placement of color values.

Check Point: Size Comparison

Slight inaccuracies multiply if not caught and corrected. After two small triangles (#3) have been sewn to small square (#2), *compare* size with triangle (#5). They should be equal.

The Ohio Star

- ☐ A block that is a recognized favorite. Block dates back to mid-1700's.
- ☐ Cut *triangle* with longest side running with the grainline to avoid ruffled *bias outer edge*.
- ☐ A dark background with a light design element is often unexpected and successful.
- ☐ Star can be cut from one fabric or many. Color value of star points must be similar or star design will be lost.

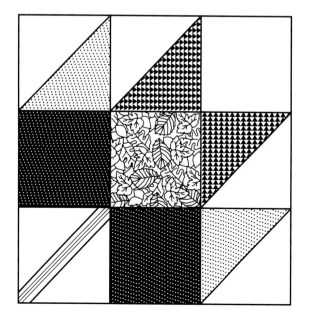

Maple Leaf

- ☐ Works up well as a Scrap Block.
- ☐ *Applique Stem* to block before piecing.
  - • Cut a 1″ by 6″ strip for stem.
  - • *Fold* raw edges to center.
  - • *Press.*
  - • *Stitch* on edges *or* use invisible blind hem. (Lesson 4)
- ☐ Use *free motion quilting* for leaf veins.

Speed Piecing

Be alert to repeating shapes and save time!

If a block has many *identically* pieced squares or rectangles, time can be saved by *speed piecing*.

In *54-40* or *Fight*, there are *ten* identical *sets of squares*. These can easily and accurately be *speed pieced*.

Instead of cutting individual squares and piecing them one by one, two fabric strips can be joined.

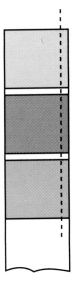

Bird of Paradise, page 42, uses a slightly different method of speed piecing squares.

One fabric *remains constant* while the joining squares are cut from a variety of fabrics. The individual fabric squares are placed upon the "constant strip" and then sewn. When cut apart, the rectangles will have been formed.

54-40 or Fight

☐ *Speed piece* identical square units.
☐ *Piece* squares into *units* of 4 squares.

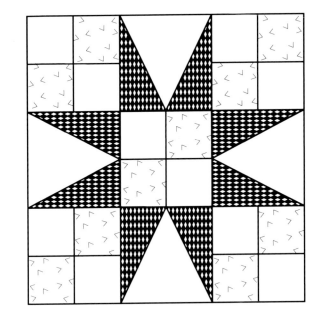

To Cut Strips For Speed Piecing:
☐ *Select* two contrasting fabrics.
☐ *Measure width* of appropriate template (#2) to determine strip *width*.
☐ *Determine strip length:* depth of template times 10, the number of desired squares.
☐ *Cut strips*.

Sew, Press, Cut, Reposition
☐ *Sew strips* with a ¼″ seam allowance.
☐ *Press* seams open.
☐ *Cut* into rectangles using ruler and rotary cutter.
☐ *Reposition* alternate rectangles, matching seam line.
☐ *Sew* into large squares.

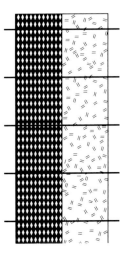

Hint:
Template For Star Point Needs Reference Marks

When sharp angles are joined, it is often difficult to align the two pieces accurately. *Reference Points* marked on the joining fabric pieces will help to create a perfectly matched seam.

On Template:
☐ *Mark* seamline angles with small ⅛" paper punched hole.

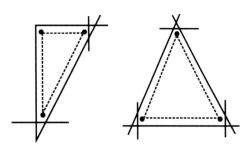

☐ *Trim* extending points to ¼".

Piecing Star Points:
☐ *Mark angles* on fabric using small hole in template and *marking pen*.
☐ Sew *one star point* to *background*, matching *marked angle dots*.
☐ *Press* seam open carefully.
☐ Add *other star point* to opposite side of *background* fabric.
☐ *Press* seam open.
☐ *Compare* size of square to *unit block*.

Bird of Paradise

☐ Like 54-40 or Fight with altered color placement.
☐ Follow *speed piecing* technique on page 41.
☐ Follow template and piecing suggestions for 54-40 or Fight.

The Rail Fence uses *speed piecing* techniques almost entirely.

Rail Fence

☐ Select 4 contrasting fabrics.
☐ *Cut* into 1½" strips the width of the fabric.
☐ *Sew* 4 strips together creating 1 long piece of "fabric."

☐ *Press* seams open or to one side.
☐ *Cut* fabric strip *into squares* using 9 Patch unit block template, (4½").

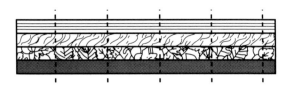

☐ *Sew*, alternating direction of square.

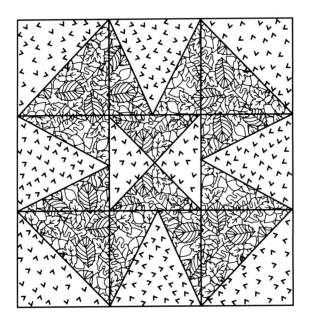

Double Z

] This unique design is based on two of the templates used in 54-40 or Fight.

] This block can be "colored" in many different ways.

Union

40 + Pieces

] For the quiltmaker who really enjoys piecing.

] This block features a unique division of the 9 patch.

Decorative Stripes

Working with *decorative* or *floral* stripes adds an element of fun and excitement to a quilt. The more you work with stripes the more possibilities you can imagine.

A *stripe* is used in Jacob's Ladder. When using a stripe in a repeating position, all stripe pieces should be cut identically.

Cutting Stripes

☐ *Place template* on lengthwise grain of decorative stripe, centering template on attractive part of design. (Use double stick tape on back of template to secure during cutting.)

☐ *Cut* piece using rotary cutter or scissors.

☐ *Use cut piece* as template for other like pieces. All striped pieces will then be *identical*.

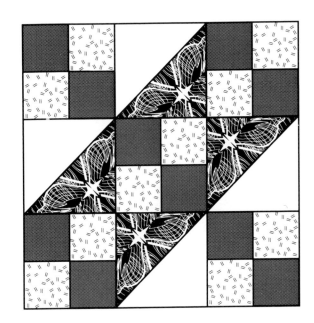

Jacob's Ladder

☐ *Speed piece* small square units.

☐ *Cut* four *identical* triangles from striped fabric.

☐ *Cut* four remaining triangles.

☐ *Piece design*.

**Arizona
45 Pieces**

Card Trick

This intriguing block requires only two triangle templates and simple piecing.

Block will be: cut, arranged, pieced into units, pieced into rows, rows joined into block.

More exciting ways to use striped fabric will be explored in the Card Trick.

Cutting and *Alignment*:

The *striped card* will be cut using 4 large triangles to align striped fabric into an attractive square. Two

of the triangles will *later* be *recut* using small (#6 template. The trimmed portion will be *discarded*.

To cut one card from striped fabric:

☐ Place long side of *large triangle* template (#5 along length of stripe. Cut *one*.

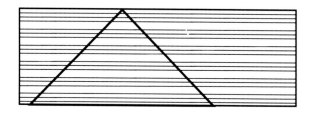

☐ *Use* cut triangle to cut 3 more identical pieces
☐ To make sure stripes fall properly, *temporarily* ar range pieces to form *square*.

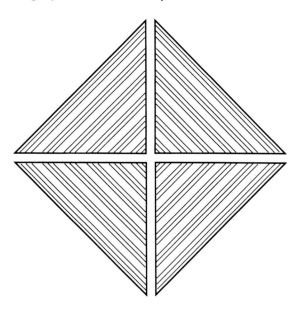

☐ *Recut 2 large triangles* into smaller triangles b placing small template on large *cut triangle* Discard *small waste* triangles.

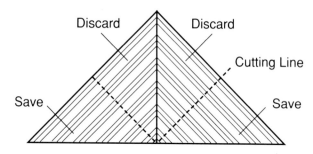

☐ *Cut* other fabrics.
☐ *Layout* entire block.
☐ Piece in *rows*.

Note: Fabrics with a decided vertical pattern shou be cut like the striped fabric for best visu presentation.

Creative Color Placement

All of the blocks presented so far have been *the traditional patterns*, designs passed down from generation to generation by word of mouth and scrap of paper. Often the very coloring in each piece was designated as being "the one" to use. Eventually these beautiful patterns were documented and compiled in books for all quiltmakers to use.

By using the traditional patterns, there is an instant bond with other quiltmakers who recognize the block and can call it by name.

This is indeed fun and part of the joy of quiltmaking.

However, quiltmaking is also a *creative process*. If you choose to recolor a design in a given block, you do not need *permission. Just do it.*

Pinwheel and Squares is a fairly new block, having been designed in 1980 by Marcia Assmundstadt, and appearing first in Jinny Beyer's, *The Quilter's Album of Blocks and Borders*. It is purposely *uncolored* for you to play with.

Pinwheel and Squares

Creative Designing: Color Placement

☐ *Trace* off several copies of the design.
☐ *Color* in design possibilities.
☐ *Piece* the design you like best.

The Quilt Backing

Total Backing Fabric Required	
Twin	7½ yards
Double/Queen	11 yards
King	12 yards
See Appendix For Complete Details	

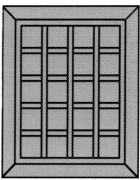

Back Of Quilt

To be *a quilt*, by the definition of the word, a *design* must be sandwiched with a layer of *batting* placed over a *backing* fabric and held together with stitches. The pieced blocks are about ready to qualify.

The *backing fabric* that you purchased must cover the back of all the blocks plus the back of the sashing that you will choose later on. If your plan includes borders, fabric must also be allowed to cover the back of the borders.

The *total backing fabric* will be divided into:
☐ fabric for the back of the quilt blocks,
☐ fabric for the back of the sashing,
☐ fabric for the back of the borders, (optional).

The fabric for the back of the blocks will be used immediately. The remaining backing fabric will be set aside, labeled and used for the finishing of the quilt.

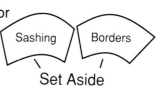

Set Aside

Dividing The Backing Fabric		
	Back of Blocks	Set Aside Yardage
Twin	3¼ yards	4¼ yards
Double/Queen	3¼ yards	7¾ yards
King	3½ yards	8½ yards

The Back of the Blocks

The fabric for the back of the blocks will be made into squares. Since the quilt backing may draw up just slightly during quilting, the squares will be cut 13″ x 13″ to allow a little *squirm room*.

Cut 13″ squares —
For *twin, double, queen*: 16
For *King*: 21

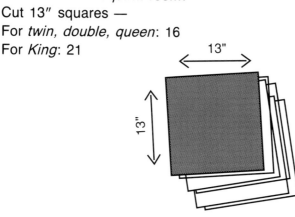

Four of the quilt blocks require a little extra working room: Log Cabin, Diagonal String, Clam Shell and Crazy Patch. 15″ backing squares will be prepared for these blocks. These will later be trimmed to 12½″.

All sizes: 4 squares: 15″ x 15″.

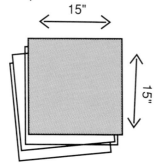

Tear Backing Fabric Into Strips
Cut Into Squares

Fabrics will first be torn into long 13″ strips. This is the easiest way to get straight yardage strips.

Most fabrics will tear on the lengthwise grain without a problem. Fabrics with a definite vertical pattern should be *evaluated* to make sure that the *pattern* runs *with* the grainline.

After the strips have been torn, they will be cut in the other direction to form squares.

To *tear* the *backings*:
☐ Tear off the selvage and discard.
☐ Measure 13″ across fabric.
☐ *Snip* into fabric to start tearing.
☐ Measure 13″ more, *snip* again.
☐ Measure 15″ and *snip* again.

☐ Gently tear the 13″ strips the length of the fabric
☐ Tear the 15″ strip 45″.

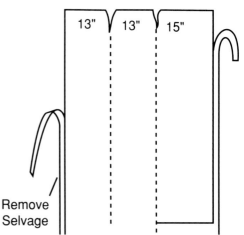

Use the rotary cutter and grid to cut the strips into 13″ squares.

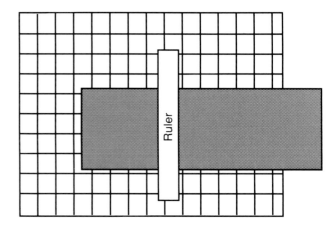

Hint: It is a good idea to cut a few extra *backings* just in case you want to make an extra block or two for "substitutes."

By having *torn* two sides and *cut* two sides you will be able to determine lengthwise grain versus crosswise grain when assembling the blocks. The *torn* edges are the *lengthwise* grain.

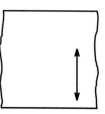

See Appendix A for cutting layout and diagram

The Batting

Batting is the filling in a quilt. It gives dimension to the quilt as well as warmth. Cotton, poly/cotton, polyester, silk and wool battings are all available. In addition the battings come in high loft, regular loft and low loft. Each has its own advantages and disadvantages. Try them all in different projects and form *your own* opinions.

Regular loft, glazed polyester batting works very well with block-by-block construction. The strong, cohesive fibers maintain their shape with minimal quilting. The batting surface is smooth, even and will not migrate through the fabric. It is washable and will not shift during quilting.

The batting comes packaged in a snug roll. This roll should be opened to allow batting to relax before cutting.

Batting squares will be cut just a bit larger than 12″. An individual *floor tile* measures 12″ and makes a good template for cutting batting as well as for pattern drafting. You don't need to be too exact when cutting batting as you want the squares of batting a tad larger than 12″ anyway.

Four layers of batting can be cut at once with the rotary cutter. Refold the batting if necessary to align edges.

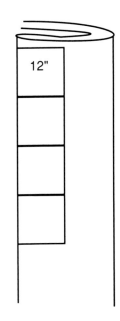

- ☐ Lay batting on cutting board.
- ☐ Use 12″ floor tile as template.
- ☐ Cut with rotary cutting wheel.
- ☐ Cut along the length of batting to save remaining length of batting for long strips needed later.
- ☐ Cut: 16–12″ squares for twin (21-King)
       4–15″ squares for any size quilt

Note: *Batting* is cut *smaller than* block design to eliminate bulk in the seam allowance line.

Quilt Sandwiches

The finished block designs will now be made into *quilt sandwiches* in preparation for quilting.

To Make A Quilt Sandwich:
- ☐ *Press* backing square.
- ☐ *Place* right side down.
- ☐ *Center Batting* on wrong side of backing square.
- ☐ *Place* pressed quilt block on batting, right side up.
- ☐ *Smooth.*
- ☐ *Press gently* on quilt block side with a warm iron.
- ☐ *Secure* with about 5 pins.

The sandwich can be pressed lightly as long as the iron does not touch the batting. Pressing does not harm the batting and it helps to hold the three layers together during quilting.

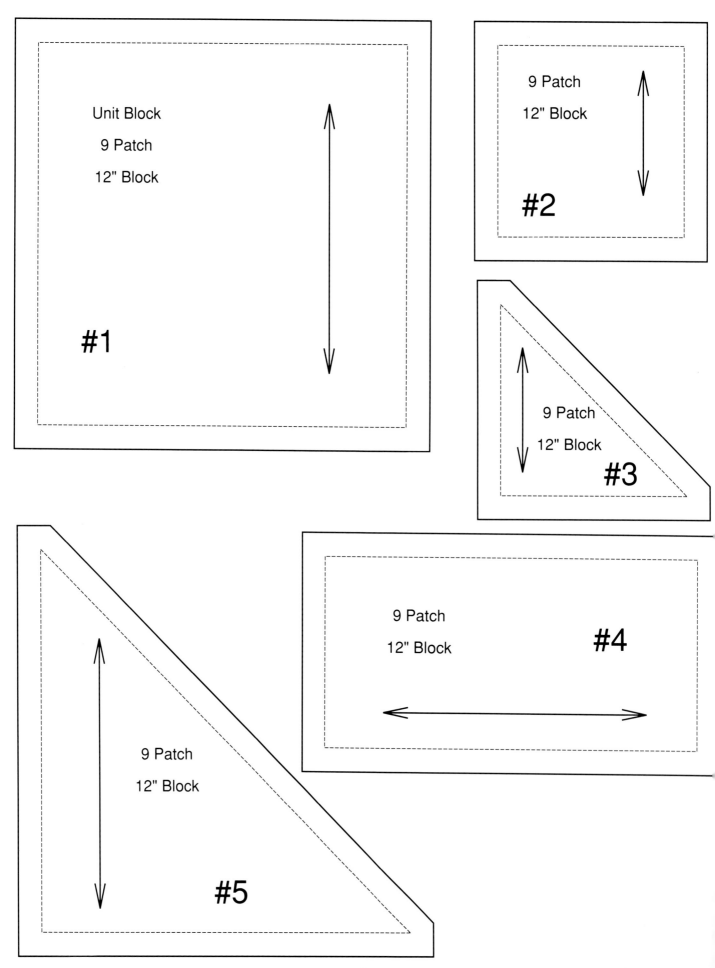

Unit Block

9 Patch

12" Block

#1

9 Patch

12" Block

#2

9 Patch

12" Block

#3

9 Patch

12" Block

#4

9 Patch

12" Block

#5

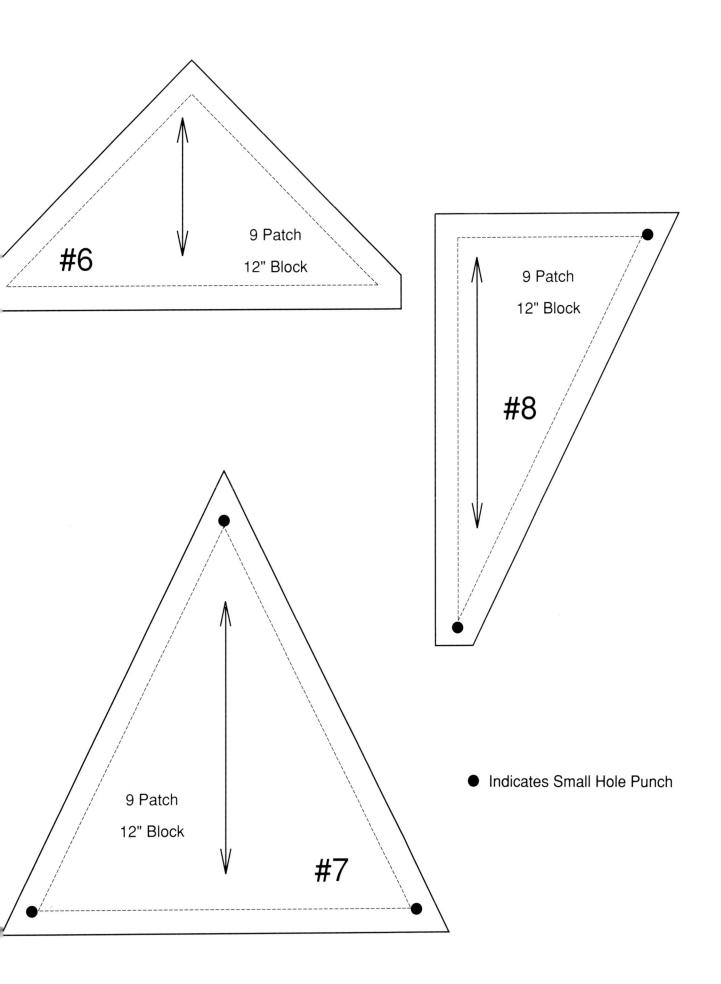

#6

9 Patch

12" Block

#8

9 Patch

12" Block

9 Patch

12" Block

#7

● Indicates Small Hole Punch

49

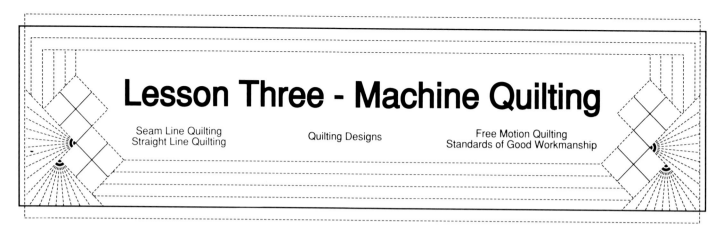

Lesson Three - Machine Quilting

Seam Line Quilting
Straight Line Quilting

Quilting Designs

Free Motion Quilting
Standards of Good Workmanship

Machine Quilting

The beauty of a block increases with each step of the quiltmaking process. Quilting adds the finishing touch to a design. It can make patterns leap from the surface as well as push a fabric quietly into the background. Quilting gives depth, texture and interest to a block.

Goal:

Quilt all 10 blocks

Skills:

Stitching in the seam line
Straight quilting lines
Other quilting designs
Free motion quilting
Adding texture to fabrics

Stitching In The Seam Line

Quilting skills are easily acquired. Start gently and let your imagination be your guide. Initially all blocks can be stitched in the seamline. Later on more quilting can be added if desired.

Hang the completed blocks on the viewing board. They may call to you for more quilting as time passes. Give rise to all your creative energy. Have *fun*, and dare to be different!

A General But Flexible Rule To Remember

Stitching around a design. . .
visually moves the design *forward*.
Stitching on the background areas. . .
visually moves the space *back*.

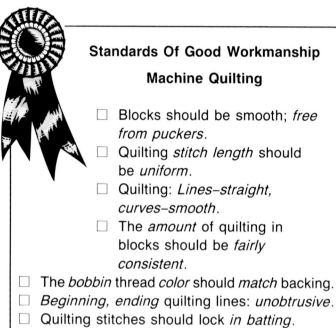

Standards Of Good Workmanship

Machine Quilting

☐ Blocks should be smooth; *free from puckers*.
☐ Quilting *stitch length* should be *uniform*.
☐ Quilting: *Lines–straight, curves–smooth*.
☐ The *amount* of quilting in blocks should be *fairly consistent*.
☐ The *bobbin* thread *color* should *match* backing.
☐ *Beginning, ending* quilting lines: *unobtrusive*.
☐ Quilting stitches should lock *in batting*.
☐ All *marking lines* should be removed.

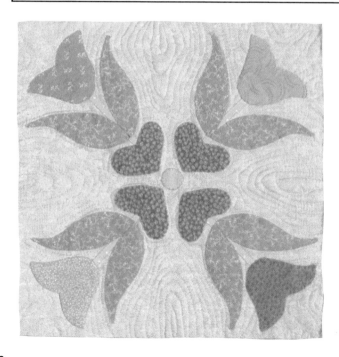

Seam Line Quilting

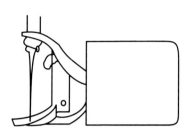

☐ *Even feed foot* suggested.
☐ *Invisible* monofilament thread *or* regular thread in medium gray.
☐ *Bobbin* thread color to *match backing*.
☐ 9 stitches per inch.

Seamline quilting holds the three layers of the quilt together while giving definition to the design elements. The quilting itself is virtually invisible from the *top* of the quilt.

Seamline quilting offers an easy quilting option for the beginning quiltmaker. *Confidence* and a *desire to experiment* with other quilting ideas will develop with experience.

The even feed foot is fairly new to home sewers. It is a box-like foot generally available as an extra accessory. It has moveable "dogs" that drop in between stitches and literally *walk* along *on* the quilt surface holding the three layers in position. The foot was originally designed to sew plaids without having to first pin them together.

The even foot feed is recommended for a smooth quilted surface and back. It is also invaluable during the final quilt finishing.

Monofilament nylon thread (.004) or *invisible thread* comes in smoke or clear. It is practically invisible so top thread color does not have to be changed frequently. It is ideal for quilting blocks containing several colors. *Top tension* of machine may have to be loosened *slightly* to balance the heavier weight thread in the bobbin. (I use it only as a top thread, but it can be used in the bobbin as well.)

Medium gray thread used in the machine needle is also an option for quilting in the seam line if the monofilament thread does not work well in your particular machine. It blends well with most fabrics. Bobbin thread should match the backing.

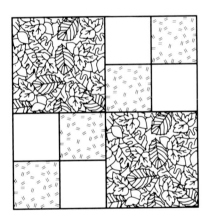

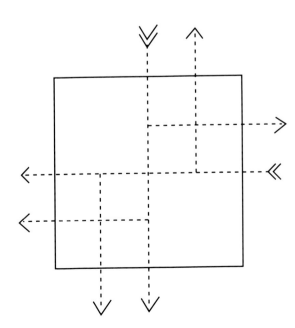

Starting and Stopping Quilting Lines

Seam allowances do not need to be left unquilted . . . as they will be covered with the sashing during the finishing.

Anchor stitching: The *long, straight* lines of seam line quilting are done first to *anchor* and *stabilize* the three layers of the quilt block. Stitching may go from one edge of the block to the other. Thread ends may be trimmed.

Diagonal and other lines of quilting can be added next without fear of distorting block.

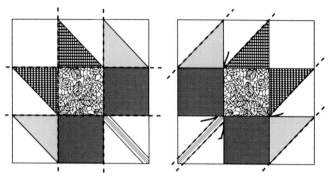

Anchor Stitching   **Diagonal Quilting**

Beginning and ending quilting threads must be *fastened* or *locked* if they originate or terminate in the middle of a block.

☐ If the fabric on *top* and *backing* are both busy prints, start with a few very small stitches to *lock* thread. Stitch with 9 stitches per inch.

☐ If the fabric is a solid or fairly plain fabric, stitch quilting lines and then:
  • pull beginning and ending threads to back of quilt.
  • use *self-threading needle*.
  • take a small backstitch and work threads into the batting.

Hint: to pull threads to back, pull on bobbin thread. It will create a small loop which is the top thread. Pull the loop to the back.

Back Of Block

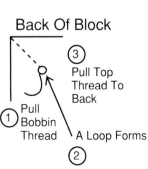

③ Pull Top Thread To Back

① Pull Bobbin Thread

A Loop Forms

②

Quilting in the seamline around the *total design* adds strength to the design.

In *Card Trick*, the design is made of many pieces. Stitching in the seamline around the complete *card* emphasizes the design. Stitching in every seamline would *fragment* the design.

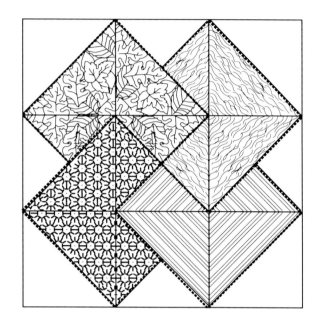

This design requires extra pinning and care in quilting as all of the lines will be quilted on the bias.

Seamline quilting can be the only quilting done on a block or it can be just the beginning. Now the quilt sandwich is stable. It is held together for further quilting by hand or machine.

Be creative and plan stitching lines that will make your blocks individual and attractive.

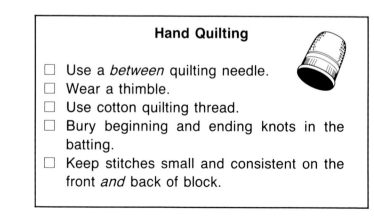

Hand Quilting

☐ Use a *between* quilting needle.
☐ Wear a thimble.
☐ Use cotton quilting thread.
☐ Bury beginning and ending knots in the batting.
☐ Keep stitches small and consistent on the front *and* back of block.

Straight Line Quilting

Straight line quilting can follow the design or divide the block geometrically.

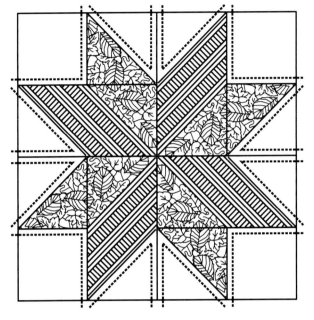

Star Flower

Outline quilting follows a design element and is stitched "a presser foot away" from the seamline eliminating the need to mark the *quilting* line on the fabric.

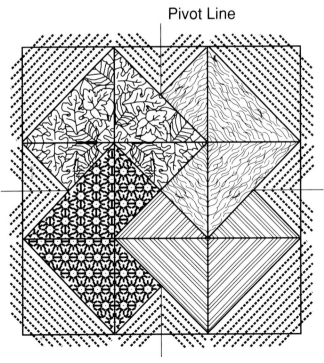

Card Trick

Echo quilting uses the presser foot as a guide and continues with rows of stitching ¼" apart.

Pivot Lines

When quilting changes direction:
- ☐ Draw a pivot line.
- ☐ Use disappearing marker.
- ☐ Quilt to pivot line.
- ☐ Pivot.
- ☐ Finish quilting line.

Virgina Star
Designed by Hazel Carter

Hint: *Do not* attempt to quilt next to the *outside seam allowance* line as this may look uneven after blocks are placed in quilt.

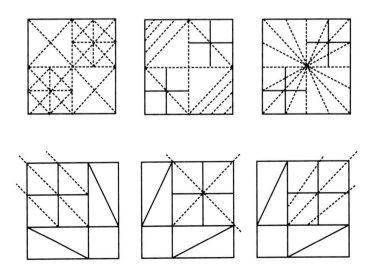

Geometric Divisions For Quilting Possibilities

Quilting Designs

Quilting designs can be pulled from designs in the fabric.

- ☐ Look for designs in the fabric. In Card Trick the pieced stripe produces a stylized heart which can be used repeatedly as a quilting design or motif.
- ☐ Draw several of these hearts onto freezer paper. These will become quilting templates.
- ☐ Position freezer paper template where desired.
- ☐ Press in place with warm iron.
- ☐ Quilt around motif.
- ☐ Remove freezer template to save or reuse.

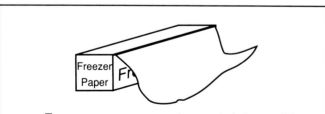

Freezer paper can be cut into quilting templates. The shiney, waxed side can be ironed onto fabric surface.

The design can either be stitched *around* the template, or the design can be lightly *marked* with a *disappearing pen*, template removed and the design stitched.

Freezer paper templates are reusable.

Quilting designs can relate to the theme of the quilt.
- ☐ Choose a simple design: heart, flower, shell.
- ☐ Use it repeatedly.
- ☐ Make your own quilting templates from freezer paper or plastic.
- ☐ Purchase commercial quilting template, if desired.

Free Motion Quilting

Free motion quilting is done without a presser foot or marking lines. *Background* areas are filled with stitching, adding depth and interest to a block. It is your free spirit dancing across the blocks. If you like to experiment, you'll *love* this!!

Free motion quilting adds your signature to the quilt. Like penmanship, no two people do free motion quilting exactly alike. Messages, dates and family names can be quilted into the quilt hidden among the other stitching lines.

- ☐ Drop or cover *feed dogs*.
  (Consult your sewing machine manual. If your machine can make a buttonhole, it probably has a way to cover or drop the feed dogs.)
- ☐ Use a darning foot or darning spring.

The *darning foot* or *darning spring* holds the fabric to the bed of the machine while the stitch is being formed. After the stitch is made the foot comes up to allow free movement of the fabric.

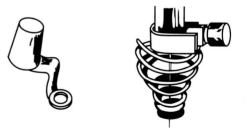

- ☐ Use a 7″ spring hoop until you gain experience.

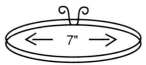

In free motion quilting, *you* are in charge. When the feed dogs are disengaged, the fabric does not move by itself. The *stitch length* is determined by the *speed* of the motor and the *rate* at which fabric is moved.

☐ *Rapid movement* produces a long stitch.
☐ *Slow movement* produces a small stitch.

The motor should run *fast*; the fabric should *glide* slowly and easily producing small, even stitches.

The fabric must be held flat on the bed of the machine or skipped stitches will result.

A spring hoop will keep fabric flat and taut against the bed of the machine. This enables the quilter to move the fabric in an even, graceful manner.

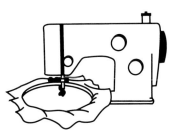

The fabric can also be ''hand held'' flat to the machine. A flat hand is heavy, however, and that makes graceful fabric movement difficult.

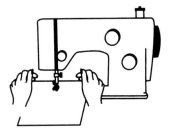

Thumb tension on either side of the quilt block can be used instead of the hoop for an easy gliding motion.

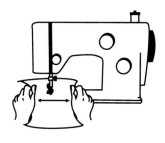

Keep lower edge of block *parallel* with front of sewing machine.

Move the block *forward and backward* or *side to side* or in a small *circular patch. Do not turn* the block *round and round* like a steering wheel.

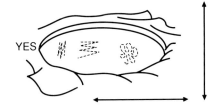

Another Ditty To Sing:
Fast goes the motor . . .
Slow and graceful moves the block!

Practice Makes Perfect . . .

☐ Write your name several times until the letters smooth out and the jerky lines disappear.
☐ Practice making big, round circles.
☐ Practice figure 8's and small circles.

Meander stitching is free motion quilting in which curving lines *meander* across the background without crossing or touching one another.
Set your mind to it and you can do it.
Say to yourself: ''I am going to make lines that curve around but do not cross any other lines!'' Make up a little ditty:
''Curve around but don't cross over!''

As silly as this may seem, a mind set helps the flow. Without a stated direction, the stitching will soon grind to a halt.

Other Meander Mind Sets –

Big Curves, Don't Cross

Mini-Curves, Don't Cross

Curve and Cross

All Circle

Straight 'n Straights

Relaxed Echos

Long Loops

Change A Shape

Connecting Flowers

The world is full of shapes that can be quilted.

Leaf Veins

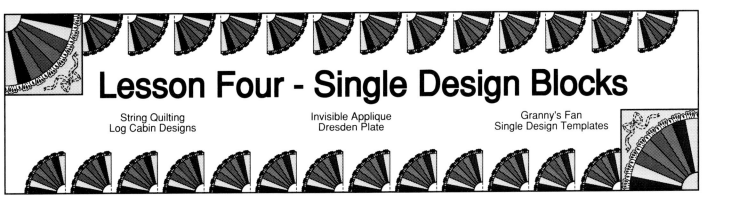

Lesson Four - Single Design Blocks

String Quilting
Log Cabin Designs

Invisible Applique
Dresden Plate

Granny's Fan
Single Design Templates

You are moving right along. If you have followed the suggested pace, you have finished half of the blocks. Have you noticed how much easier it is at this point to choose your colors? Your confidence is building.

The next four blocks require very little quilting. You will be surprised at the speed in which these lovely blocks can be completed.

The blocks in this chapter are *not pieced* like the 4 Patch and 9 Patch block designs. The technique used to complete the *string quilted* blocks and the Log Cabin designs is called *Quilt-As-You-Go*. As the pieces are sewn to one another the block is also being quilted, saving you one step.

String quilting is probably the easiest technique in the whole quilt. This type of quilting is popular in quilted clothing as well as in decorator items for the household.

The Log Cabin blocks are presented in two sizes; a 12″ block will complete a single design. For the ambitious quiltmaker, four 6″ blocks can be assembled and sewn to complete the 12″ block.

The *Dresden Plate* block has always been a favorite with traditional quiltmakers. The machine techniques create petals with lovely sharp points or smooth curves depending upon your preference. An entire quilt can easily be made with just this block.

Granny's Fan has also been a traditional favorite.

Goal: *Complete 4 one patch designs.*
Skills:
   String Quilting
   Applique
   Marking Designs

String Quilting

These blocks use narrow strips of fabric and the Quilt-As-You-Go technique. As the strips are sewn in place, the block is simultaneously quilted. Each strip is sewn down and secured by the next strip.

Goal: *Make one string quilted block*

A 15″ backing and a 15″ piece of batting will be used as the foundation for the string quilted block and the Log Cabin block. These two blocks tend to squirm a little in construction and the extra inches are for your protection. They will later be squared and trimmed to 12½″. Save the trimmed scraps for your Crazy Patch.

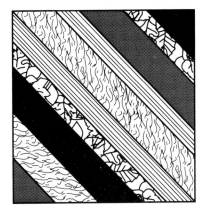

String Quilting

Fabrics: Use a wide variety of prints and solids, lights, mediums and darks to make this block. These strips are called *Strings*.

Cut: 10 to 12 one and a half inch strips, the width of the fabric. Use the rotary cutter.
Prepare: Use a 15″ backing, batting sandwich.
Sew: Use even feed foot.

- ☐ Make 15" backing and batting sandwich.
- ☐ Place the first strip diagonally across the batting, ends touching opposite corners, strip right side up.
- ☐ Trim strip to end of block.
- ☐ Lay second strip on top of first strip, right sides together.
- ☐ Sew right edge with a ¼" seam through batting and backing.
- ☐ Turn top strip right side up.
  - • Trim strip end.
  - • Finger crease seam line.
  - • Pin raw edge in place to hold strip flat momentarily.

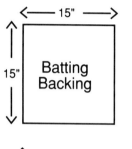

- ☐ Place next strip on top of previous strip, right sides together.
  - • Reposition pins.
  - • Sew, turn, finger crease.
- ☐ Continue in this manner until one half of square is filled with strips. Repeat for the other half.
- ☐ Carefully trim block to 12½".
- ☐ Save scraps for Crazy Patch.

Variety: Strips can be made to look different widths.
- ☐ Position new strip, with raw edges parallel to lower strip.
- ☐ Allow lower strip to extend beyond new strip.
- ☐ Sew, right sides together, narrowing lower strip.

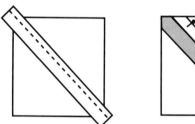

Variable Width String

Angled strips make an interesting variation in string quilting.
- ☐ Use 1½" strips.
- ☐ Position first strip, right side up.
- ☐ Place next strip so that edges are not even with the raw edge of previous string.
- ☐ Sew.
- ☐ Trim excess fabric from lower strip.
- ☐ Turn top strip to final position.
  - • finger press
  - • pin edges in place
- ☐ Repeat with alternate angle.

Irregular String

The Log Cabin Block

The Log Cabin block is a study of contrast—light and dark. It calls for carefully graded values and precise sewing. The strong diagonal line separates the sunshine, light fabrics, from the shadow, dark fabrics. The square in the center is traditionally red or yellow to suggest fire or smoke rising from a chimney.

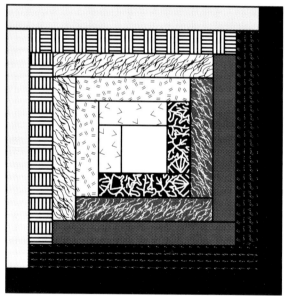

By squinting at the fabrics in a dim light, you can more easily sort the values from light to dark. I find that early morning is a good time for this as the eyes are only partially opened anyway.

Some fabrics contain sharply contrasting values in the same fabric. For example, the black and white tile design has sharply contrasting values which do not seem to blend together. This type of fabric will always remain spotty and not read properly. Eliminate this type of fabric in the Log Cabin.

Fabric swatches can be photocopied, reducing them to black and white or gray scale. Color values then become apparent.

Goal: *Make one Log Cabin block*

- [ ] Select: 5 graduated light fabrics; 5 graduated dark fabrics; 1 chimney fabric (possibly red or yellow)
- [ ] Arrange fabrics from light to dark.
- [ ] Cut Chimney 2½".
- [ ] Cut 1½" strips across the grain using the rotary cutter. 4 lights and 4 darks.
- [ ] Cut darkest light and darkest dark 2".

Note: The stitching and turning technique has a tendency to shrink the logs. The wider outside strips will bring the block up to size.

Construction:

Make a 15" backing/batting sandwich.

Logs will be added around the center square in clockwise direction alternating 2 matching lights and 2 matching darks.

Find the center of the batting by drawing diagonal lines across batting with vanishing pen.

Chimney corners will be placed to touch lines.

Hint: *Accuracy pays dividends.*

- [ ] Lay lightest strip on right side of chimney square, right sides together.
- [ ] Start sewing ¼" from top of strip. Stop ¼" short of bottom of square. (This eliminates stitching spurs on the back.)
- [ ] Secure threads by bringing threads up to

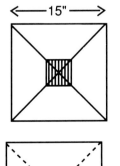
← 15" →
Sew To Here
Cut Here
Tie Threads

the top of the block. Tie off.
- [ ] Trim strip to equal length of square.
- [ ] Turn strip into position.
  - Finger crease seam line.
  - Pin to hold strip in place.
- [ ] Sew second strip the width of center square plus 1st log.

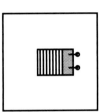

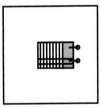

Hint: Use *small ruler* to make sure center is exactly square.

- [ ] Continue adding 2 darks and 2 lights.
- [ ] Trim to 12½" square.

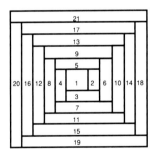

If You Have A Limited Number Of Fabrics:

- [ ] Arrange fabrics from light to dark on one side and arrange fabrics from dark to light on other side.
- [ ] Use one fabric for one side of Log Cabin and grade fabrics from light to dark for second side.

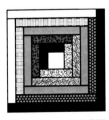

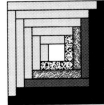

Mini Log Cabin

Assembly line piecing is efficient and accurate. This Mini Log Cabin block is pieced without batting or backing. Four 6″ Log Cabin blocks will be joined to make the quilt block. It will then be sandwiched and quilted in the seam lines.

Mini Log Cabin Blocks
Assembly Line Piecing

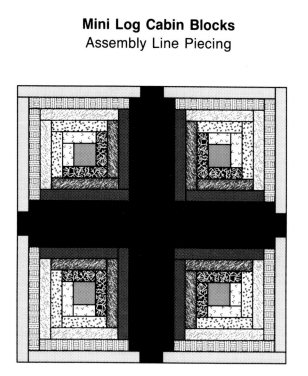

The sunshine and shadow effect becomes more apparent when four blocks are joined.

Cut one inch strips:
Cut 5 light and 5 dark strips
Cut 4 centers: 1½″ square.

Sew 4 Log Cabins
☐ Lay 4 centers upon lightest light strip. Sew right edge with ¼″ seam.
☐ Cut lights equal in size to centers.
☐ Open pair and press seams away from center
☐ Lay combined squares on same light and sew
☐ Continue sewing 4 Log Cabins in this manner until each side has 5 logs.

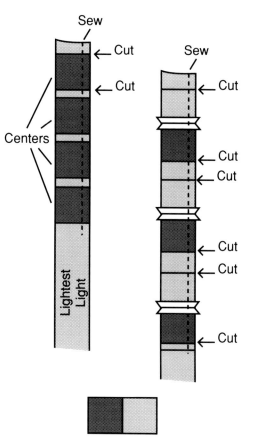

Join blocks in desired pattern:
☐ darks to the center
☐ lights to the center
☐ 4 blocks positioned identically

Layer with batting, backing.
Quilt in the seam lines.

Invisible Applique

Applique is used to apply one piece of fabric to another. In the Dresden Plate, the pieced plate will be appliqued to a foundation fabric.

In applique for quilts, I like to have the raw edges turned under *first* before the fabric is appliqued. This gives a stronger edge and is more in keeping with the traditional applique. It is also easier as there is no concern over ravels and exposed raw edges.

There are several methods of machine applique that work well. Your machine will probably determine which to use.

- - - - - ^- - - - - ^- - - - - ^-

Blind Hem Applique

Blind hem applique is meant to be invisible on the surface of the quilt. Invisible nylon thread and the blind hem stitch of the machine make this possible. A machine with zig-zag capability is required.
] The needle thread will be the invisible nylon.
] The bobbin thread will match the quilt backing.
] The machine will be set for blind hem stitch
  • Set at about 40 stitches/inch (very tight stitch)
  • Set zig-zag width at 1½ (very small jump)
] The straight stitches will fall in the foundation.
] The jump-over stitches will fall in the applique.

Note: The jump-over stitch width, - - - ^-, closes as the stitch length becomes smaller. The smaller the straight machine stitches are, the tighter the jump-over stitch is. A small, close, jump-over stitch is desired.
] Blind hem applique can also be done with a decorative thread in the needle for a different effect.
] For a strong emphasis with the decorative thread, the needle can be threaded with two threads going through the same needle eye.

- - - - - - - - - - - - - - - - - -

Straight Stitch Applique

An attractive and nearly invisible applique results from stitching on the very edge of the appliqued fabric.
] Use invisible thread or a decorative thread.
] Experiment with different stitch lengths.

The Dresden Plate

The Dresden Plate block can be made easily in any size and can have either pointed or rounded petals. The ends of the petal are cut to include a facing for simple and foolproof finishing.

The Dresden Plate is a combination block. The petals are pieced into a plate and then appliqued onto a foundation.

Template for any size Dresden Plate can be drafted on typing or tracing paper using a compass:
□ Draw circle size of desired plate. Use 5½″ radius for 12″ block.
□ Use same center point, draw 1″ radius circle.
□ Divide large circle into 16ths. Fold paper into quarters. Divide one quarter in fourths.

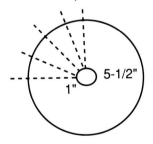

□ One section becomes pointed petal template.
  • Redraw curved outer edge to straight edge.
  • Remove the 1″ from lower edge.
  • Add ¼″ seam allowance to all sides.
  • Cut template from plastic. Label.

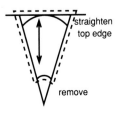

- ☐ To make rounded petal template:
  - Start with the same ¹⁄₁₆ circle section.
  - Extend long sides of petal ½″.
  - Connect extended lines with straight line.
  - Remove the 1″ from lower edge.
  - Add ¼″ seam allowance to all sides.
  - Mark fold line 1″ from top edge with seam line clips.

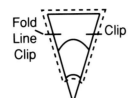

3½″ circle becomes center template.

2½″ circle becomes pressing template (Cut template from tagboard or old file folder.)

Foundation: 13″ square (¼″ squirm room has been allowed.)

Cut: 16 petals which will contrast in value with the foundation.

- ☐ Use strip cutting method with rotary cutter to save time.
  - Layer 4 fabrics.
  - Cut strip depth of petals.
  - Use template to cut petals.

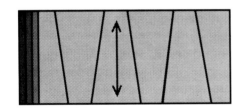

To Sew Pointed Petals:

- ☐ Fold petals in half lengthwise, right sides together.
- ☐ Chain sew across straight ends.
- ☐ Clip petals apart and trim fabric at fold. (This reduces the bulk in the point of the petal.)
- ☐ Finger press seam allowance open.
- ☐ Turn end into finished position using point turner.
- ☐ Press.

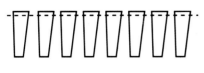

To Sew Rounded Petals:

- ☐ Fold over 1″ of petal tip, right sides together.
- ☐ Mark curved stitching line on "Fold Over" using curved pressing template as a guide.
- ☐ Sew on marked curve.
- ☐ Trim curve to ⅛″.
- ☐ Clip to seam line.
- ☐ Turn carefully forming smooth curve.
- ☐ Press well over pressing template, rolling seam line slightly to back.

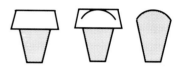

Sew 16 petals:

- ☐ Sew 2 petals, right sides together.
  - Start ⅛″ from top edge to avoid creating thread whiskers.
  - Backstitch to fold.
  - Reverse directon.
  - Sew to end of petal.
- ☐ Join pairs, then ¼ circles, etc.

Press:

- ☐ Swirl iron, pressing seams to one side.
- ☐ Dresden plate should lie flat.

Hint: If plate does not lie flat, slight adjustments may have to be made in a few seam allowances. If so, adjust seam allowances on petals opposite each other to keep "plate" balanced.

Center pieced plate

- ☐ Mark foundation diagonals with marking pen or light creases with the iron.
- ☐ Four plate points will touch crease lines.
- ☐ Remove marking or creases lines.
- ☐ Place foundation on batting and backing.

Applique Dresden Plate:

- ☐ Use invisible thread in machine needle.
- ☐ Use blind stitch setting set at 40 stitches per inch. (very tight!)
- ☐ Quilt all layers

- Set zig-zag width at 1½. (small jump)
- Stitch around outside edge of petals.
  - Stitch with the straight stitches of the blind hem on the foundation fabric.
  - Catch "plate" with the jump-over stitch.

or

Sew on outside edge of petal with straight stitch.

Apply Center
- Cut center using cutting template.
- Run gathering stitch (6 stitches per inch) around outside edge of center.
- Place center on pressing template.
  - Pull up gathers over template.
  - Press edge.
  - Pop pressing template from center.
- Use invisible thread and blind hem stitch to secure center to Dresden Plate.

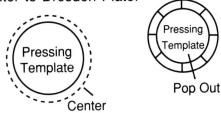

Hint: for a puffy center, first place circle of batting on pressing template. Add fabric center and gather.

Quilt
- Stitch in the seam line between petals.
- Outline quilt ¼" from outside of petals, if desired.

Granny's Fan

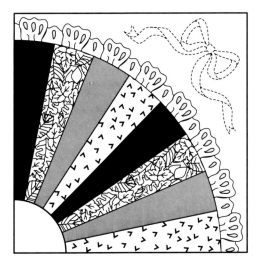

The Fan looks most natural when pieced in light and contrasting dark fabrics to represent the angles of the fan. The reverse side of a fabric often works very well to achieve the shadowed effect.

Paper Folded Templates

- Fan: Draw ¼ circle, 10" radius.
- Fan Base: Draw Base Arc 4" from center.
- Isolate Fan and Arc Sections.
  - Fan template:
    a. fold ¼ circle into 8 sections.
    b. isolate one section, add ¼" seam allowance.
  - Fan Base template: add seam allowance to ¼ circle arc.

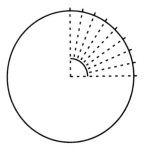

Notions: One yard lace, slightly gathered or flat.

Cut: 4 *light* wedges, 4 *dark* wedges; 1 curved fan base; 8" x 1" bias strip to match fan base; 13" foundation fabric.

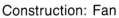

Construction: Fan
- Sew 8 Fan wedges together, alternating light and dark fabrics. Press seams to one side.
- Finish top edge of fan by sewing lace or other trim to upper edge of Fan, right sides together. Turn trim to finished position.
- Finish bottom edge of fan with lace or bias strip.

Make Quilt Sandwich: Backing, Batting, Foundation

Position Fan:
- Position base in lower corner of foundation fabric.
- Place fan on base and foundation.
- Measure distance from first petal to nearest corner.
- Measure distance from last petal to its nearest corner. They should be equal.

Sew Fan To Foundation:
- Stitch in the seam line next to lace.
- Attach lower edge of fan with invisible applique.
- Quilt in the seam line between wedges.

Quilting Design:
- Transfer design to foundation using light box and marking pen. (Lift up loose corner of foundation and place on light box.)
- Stitch marked design by hand or machine.
  - Stitch bow with feed dogs in position.
  - Drop feed dogs and use free motion quilting for lacy tendrils.
- Embellish with other embroidery stitches if desired.

A Simple Light Box

A simple light box for marking designs can be created from a clear plastic shoe or sweater box and a mechanics drop light.

Use a bold marker to trace design on paper or freezer paper. Tape design on bottom of inverted sweater box. Place light inside.

Center fabric on design. Trace with marking pen or chalk.

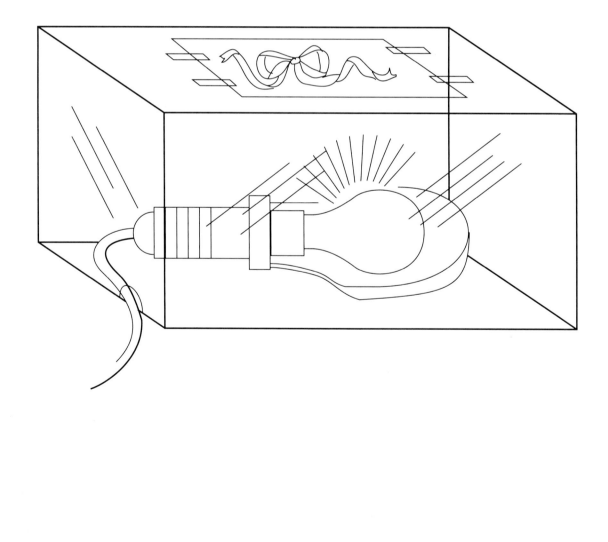

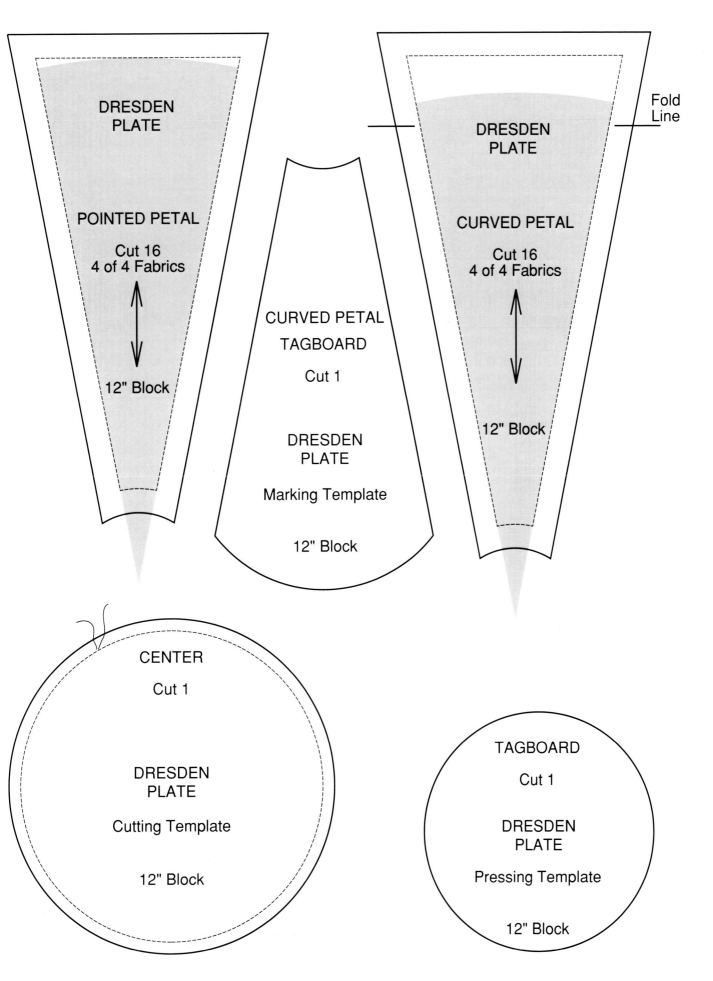

DRESDEN
PLATE

POINTED PETAL

Cut 16
4 of 4 Fabrics

12" Block

CURVED PETAL

TAGBOARD

Cut 1

DRESDEN
PLATE

Marking Template

12" Block

DRESDEN
PLATE

CURVED PETAL

Cut 16
4 of 4 Fabrics

12" Block

Fold
Line

CENTER

Cut 1

DRESDEN
PLATE

Cutting Template

12" Block

TAGBOARD

Cut 1

DRESDEN
PLATE

Pressing Template

12" Block

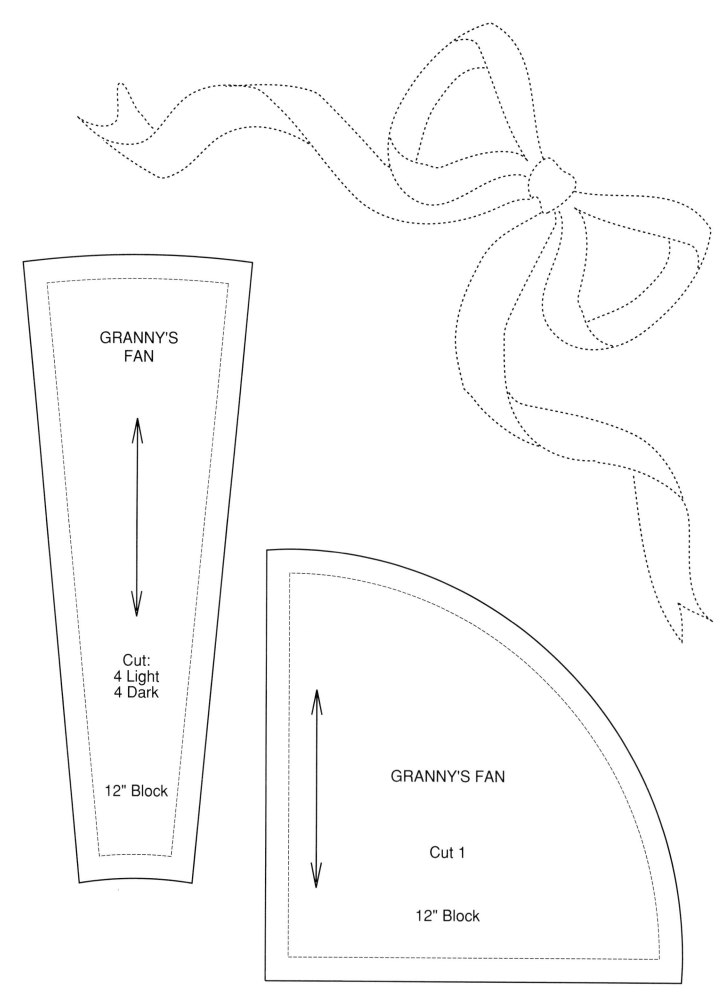

GRANNY'S
FAN

Cut:
4 Light
4 Dark

12" Block

GRANNY'S FAN

Cut 1

12" Block

Lesson Five - Five Patch Designs
Curved Patchwork

Start Arranging Your Blocks
Drafting the Five Patch
5 Patch Blocks

Speed Piecing Half Square Triangles

Appliqued Curves
Pieced Curves
Templates

The blocks for your quilt are nearing completion. You still have time to modify your color scheme if desired. Stop for a few minutes to arrange the blocks as they might be in the finished quilt. Is there anything missing? . . . Would a few dark backgrounds add a spark to the quilt? . . . Have you just found a new fabric that works well? Use it in these blocks and be sure to add it to the Clam Shell . . . Has your accent or zinger gotten out of control? If over-use has taken away its punch, find another zinger one step brighter. Add it sparingly to a few of the remaining blocks.

Appraise the blocks that you have, filling in deficits with the remaining designs.

Goal:

Make and *quilt* at least three new blocks.

Quilt additional designs on previous blocks, if desired.

Skills:

Drafting the 5 Patch
5 Patch Designs
Appliqued Curves
Pieced Curves

The Five Patch

The Five Patch blocks are well balanced as they actually have 25 divisions and a definite center square. These traditional patterns frequently have cross bars separating four rotating corner designs. This subtle sense of motion adds energy as well as asthetic beauty to the quilt.

Another Method Of Drafting

By taking the time to understand this method of drafting, you will expand your quiltmaking possibilities. Up until now you have been using *graph paper* to draft patterns when the mathematical divisions have been simple. With this method, any block can be drafted to a given size, even if that size is unusual or uneven.

Drafting The Five Patch

Since a 12″ block mathematically does not divide *evenly* by five, another method of drafting will be illustrated.

☐ Draw a 12″ square.

☐ Ask yourself: "What number larger than 12 (size of block) is divisible by 5? (5 Patch)
Answer: 15
Five goes into 15, how many times?
Answer: 3

☐ Use these figures to draw 5 Patch Grid of 25 squares.

Place one end of the long ruler in the lower left corner of the 12″ square and the 15″ mark of the ruler on the right side of the square.

Place a dot at the three inch mark. Add other dots at the 6, 9 and 12 inch marks of the ruler.

Use a T-Square to draw straight lines through dots from top to bottom of square.

Turn "grid" and repeat. You now have 25 squares. Use these squares to draw the 5 Patch templates.

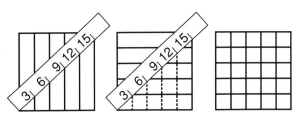

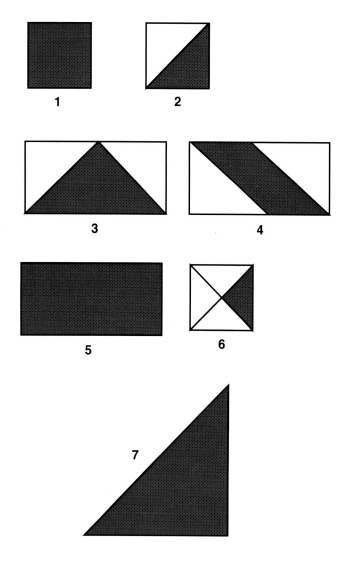

1

2

3

4

5

6

7

Make 5 Patch Templates:
- ☐ Use 5 Patch grid.
- ☐ Shade in desired patterns.
- ☐ Trace pattern piece onto graph paper.
- ☐ Add seam allowance.
- ☐ Finish templates.

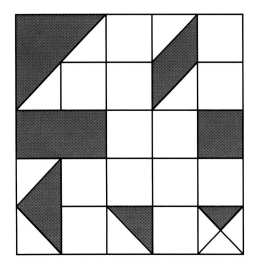

Red Cross

The four corner sections are identical. Rotate each section ¼ turn.

A crisp secondary design develops when center triangles are deepest value.

A stripe works well for the center column in the 5 Patch.

Jack In The Box

Select fabrics that will enhance the design.

A folded over design is implied. Have triangle points be fairly bold with a muted or shadowed effect in the "connecting arms" or use another fabric that will give the shadowed illusion.

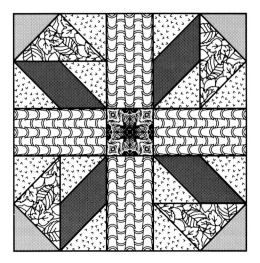

Cross and Crowns   **Duck and Ducklings**

These two 5 Patch designs are somewhat similar and make fine additions to a SAMPLER quilt.

Flying Geese

Flying Geese is similar to the other 5 Patch designs but has many repeating triangle units. *Speed piecing* these units using freezer paper can save time and energy. The bias edge of the joining triangles is stabilized by the freezer paper during sewing.

Please see speed piecing instructions on next page.

Speed Piecing With Freezer Paper – Half Square Triangles

When several identical sets of triangles appear in a block, speed piecing is a logical solution.

Two fabrics can be layered, right sides together. A grid drawn onto freezer paper and ironed onto the fabrics will be the sewing and cutting guide.

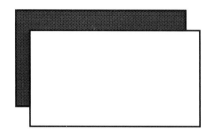

- ☐ Determine how many sets of triangles are needed.
- ☐ Select proper template.
- ☐ Draw a large right angle on a piece of 10″ x 15″ freezer paper.

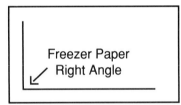

Freezer Paper
Right Angle

- ☐ Place template which includes seam allowance on freezer paper, straight sides of template touching sides of right angle.

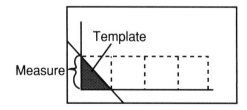

Template

Measure

- ☐ Draw diagonal line, using template for guide.
- ☐ Measure straight side of triangles.

- ☐ Draw a grid of squares using this measurement. (One grid square will yield two sets of sewn triangles.)
- ☐ Draw diagonal lines in one direction only, connecting opposite corners.

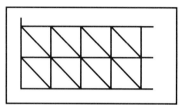

- ☐ Sew ¼″ on each side of every diagonal line.

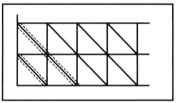

- ☐ Cut on every line.
- ☐ Remove freezer paper by tearing paper toward the center of the triangle to avoid pulling out the stitches.
- ☐ Press seams open.

Note: You will be sewing over the points of some triangles. After grid has been cut apart, these few stitches will easily be removed using seam ripper.

Curves

Curves have long been reserved for the experienced quiltmaker. Now, however, a beautiful foolproof *appliqued curve* can be made on the machine with a little help from your iron. The Clam Shell design will delight and amaze you and your friends. It will be the "attention getter" in your quilt . . . The Drunkard's Path blocks are *pieced curve* designs which add an unusual line design to a quilt.

Clam Shell

"I *know* you didn't make *that block* . . . by *machine!!*

Clam Shell is a *curved applique* block which adds color interest to a SAMPLER by coordinating all the fabrics of the quilt into one block. The blind hem and invisible thread work magic to secure the clams and to quilt the block all at one time.

This block requires 56 clam shells.

Cut: 56 clams by layering several fabrics at a time.
- ☐ Use all of your fabrics.
- ☐ Align fabric grain lines.
- ☐ Use Gingher Duckbills held perpendicular to surface to cut multi-layers with accuracy.

Note: Your fabrics should be a good mix of light, medium and dark fabrics highlighted by one or two brights and anchored by several really dark prints.

If your fabric selection is becoming depleted, *add* more fabrics now. Think ahead to the *picture blocks* and search for fabrics that will help "tell the story." Look for rooftops, bricks, sky, water. The use of realistic fabric design adds a touch of whimsy to a block.

Machine Baste Clams:
- ☐ Stitch ⅛" from outer curved edge of each calm.
- ☐ Use long stitch – 6 stitches per inch.
- ☐ Use different colors of thread in bobbin and top.
- ☐ Chain baste clams leaving 6" between clams.

- ☐ Clip clams apart.
- ☐ Pull up gathers over pressing template made of tagboard. (Bobbin threads pull easiest.)
- ☐ Set crease with spray starch.

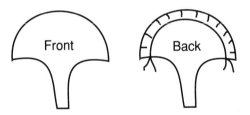

Make a 15" sandwich of *batting* and *backing*.
- ☐ Use marking pen to draw guide line across batting 3" from top.
- ☐ Start at the top. Lay a row of "touching" clams. (This will be a practice row as only the stem of these clams will show.)

- ☐ Use invisible thread and applique clams to batting using the blind hem stitch around outside edge of clams with only the grabbing stitch going into the clam.
- ☐ Lay the next rows of clams in the same manner with pressed curve positioned on stem seam allowance.
- ☐ Half clams can be used at beginning or end of rows.
- ☐ Trim the block to 12½". Save scrap for Crazy Patch.

Cut Off

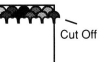

Clamshell Template:
- ☐ Use compass and graph paper.
- ☐ Draw and quarter a 3″ circle.
- ☐ Connect side and base marks with same arc.
- ☐ Add ¼″ seam allowance on all sides.

Clamshell Pressing Template (Tagboard):
- ☐ Draw 3″ Clam Shell.
- ☐ Do not add seam allowances.
- ☐ Add a handle to hold onto when pressing.

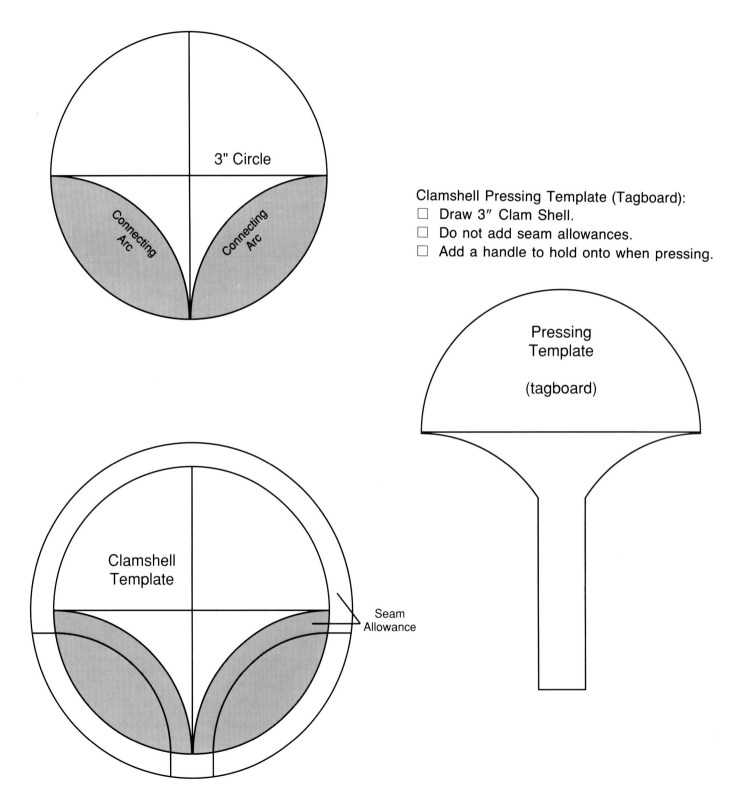

3″ Circle

Connecting Arc

Connecting Arc

Pressing Template

(tagboard)

Clamshell Template

Seam Allowance

Moon Over The Mountain – Picture Block With Curves

Use templates on page 74 or draft your own pattern:
- [ ] Draw a 12″ square:
  - Try drawing on freezer paper.
  - Use 12″ floor tile template.
- [ ] Divide diagonally into quarters.
- [ ] Draw ¾ circle, radius 2¼″.
- [ ] Isolate 3 design elements.
- [ ] Make templates adding ¼″.

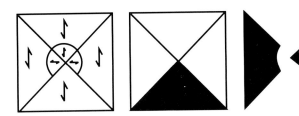

Fabrics: Choose fabrics to make a *day* or *nighttime scene*.

Piecing:
- [ ] Find the center of the moon and center of the sky.
- [ ] Pin centers together.
- [ ] Pin straight sides together near seam line.
- [ ] Turn pieces over and sew from 'sky' side with ¼″ seam allowance.

- Sew from straight side to center.
- Stop with needle down.

- Rearrange fabric.
- Sew to remaining straight side.
- [ ] Press fabric toward sky.
- [ ] Sew 2 quarters of block together.
- [ ] Sew the two halves together.

Moon Over The Mountain

Alternative Sky:
- [ ] Cut 3 sky pieces from muslin, adding ¼″ on all sides for "squirm room."
- [ ] Mark directional ray lines on muslin.
- [ ] Use irregular string quilting (1½″ strings) to fill up muslin sky pieces using directional markings as a guide.
- [ ] Start string quilting in the center of each muslin piece.
- [ ] Trim excess bulk from bottom strips.
- [ ] Recut sky using template.
- [ ] Piece to moon sections, etc.

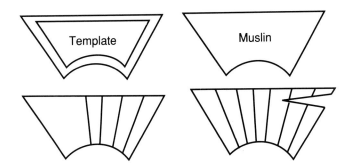

73

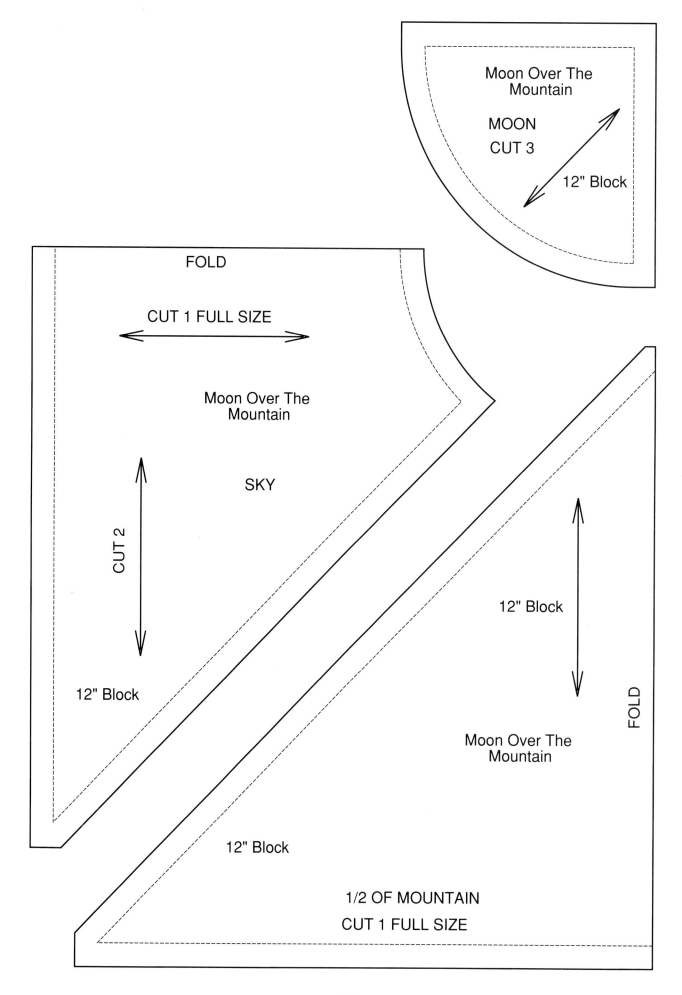

Moon Over The Mountain

MOON
CUT 3

12" Block

FOLD

CUT 1 FULL SIZE

Moon Over The Mountain

SKY

CUT 2

12" Block

12" Block

FOLD

Moon Over The Mountain

12" Block

1/2 OF MOUNTAIN

CUT 1 FULL SIZE

More Curves . . . Pieced

Variation On The Drunkard's Path Block

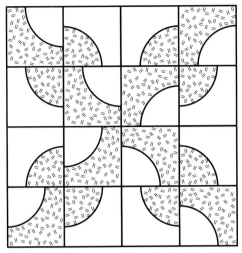

Drunkard's Path

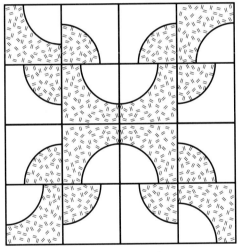

Fallen Timbers

Carolyn's Path

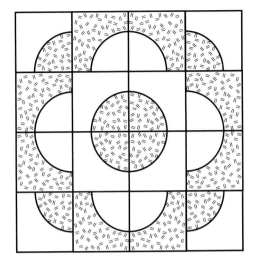

Love Ring

Two templates create these curved 4 Patch designs based on variations of the Drunkard's Path.

The *unit block* is divided by an arc which measures ⅔ of the base measurement.

Alternate arrangements of the pieced squares produce a wide variety of blocks.

Patterns on page 76.

Pattern Drafting:

☐ Draw a 3" square.
☐ Draw arc ⅔ of base. (2")
☐ Add seam allowances.

Fabrics: two *contrasting* fabrics

Cut: 8 *light* and 8 *dark* from each template. (32 pieces)

To Sew:

☐ Fold curved edges in half to determine mid-points.
☐ Pin mid-points of curves together.
☐ Pin straight edges together near seamline to properly align for sewing.

☐ Sew to mid-point pin.
☐ Rearrange fabrics without removing from machine.
☐ Finish curved seam.
☐ Correct any flat spots in curve.
☐ Press seams in either direction but *do not* press seams open.

Arrange block and sew as a 4 Patch.

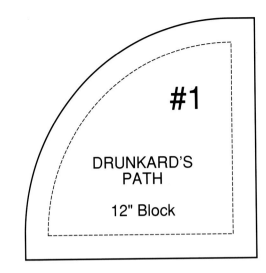

#1

DRUNKARD'S
PATH

12" Block

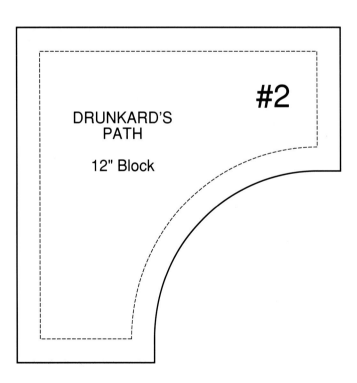

#2

DRUNKARD'S
PATH

12" Block

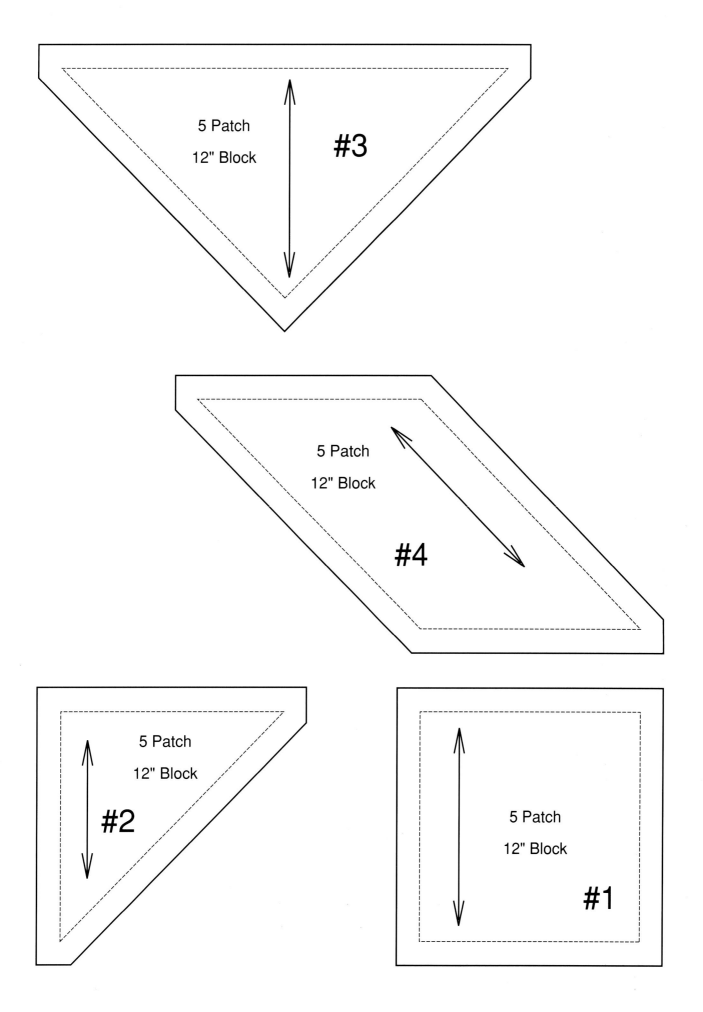

5 Patch

12" Block

#3

5 Patch

12" Block

#4

5 Patch

12" Block

#2

5 Patch

12" Block

#1

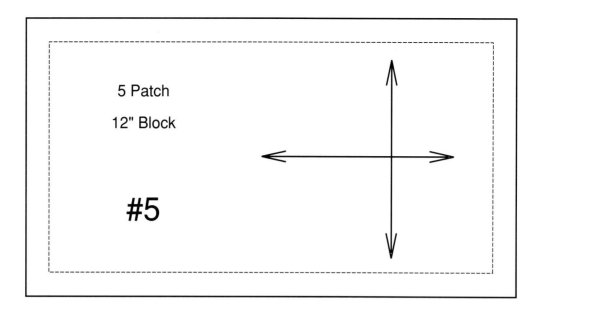

5 Patch

12" Block

#5

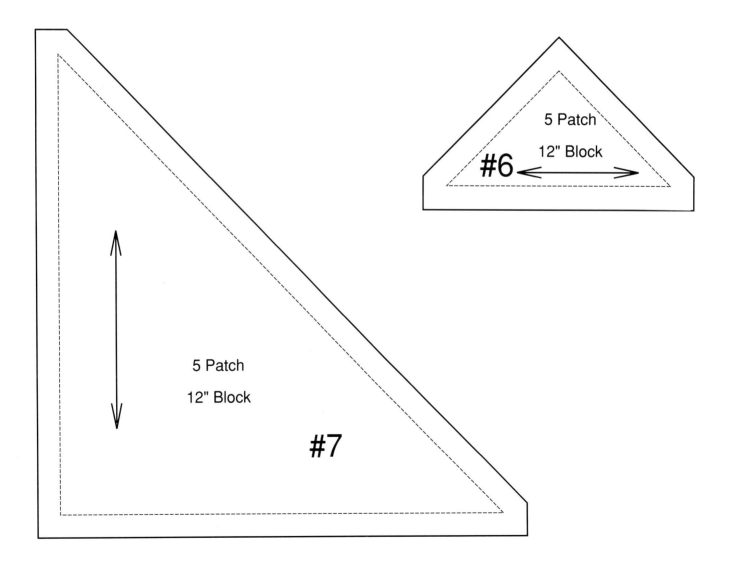

5 Patch

12" Block

#7

5 Patch

12" Block

#6

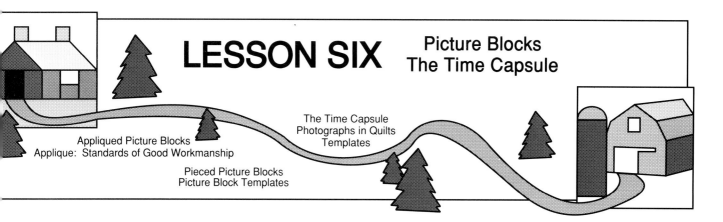

LESSON SIX

Picture Blocks
The Time Capsule

Appliqued Picture Blocks
Applique: Standards of Good Workmanship

Pieced Picture Blocks
Picture Block Templates

The Time Capsule
Photographs in Quilts
Templates

Picture blocks personalize a SAMPLER quilt. They are your children, your house and your vacation scenes embellished and decorated. Picture blocks tell the story. The special touches are the heart and soul of a quilt. This is your chance to select blocks meaningful to your family or to create original blocks of your own.

The picture blocks will be presented in two different categories. The first blocks will be appliqued. Pieces will be cut, shaped and placed upon a foundation before sewing. It is easy to modify this type of block to tell "your story."

Several pieced picture block designs are included as well as two original designs by author. Directions for you to make your own *original* blocks are included. Pieced blocks can be embellished and personalized also.

The Time Capsule or Crazy Patch is your opportunity to record your present day "history" in among the scrap fabrics of your quilt.

Goal: Personalize Quilt
   Make 3 or more blocks.
Skills: Applique
   Embellishment
   Decorative Stitching

Applique Picture Blocks

Simple shapes are the basis for applique. Coloring books, newspaper and magazine ads, children's drawings and even cereal boxes offer simple and sometimes stylized suggestions for designs. Keep the applique itself simple and embellish it with stitching and other found objects if desired.

The Sunbonnet Sue blocks cover the *principles* of *applique.*

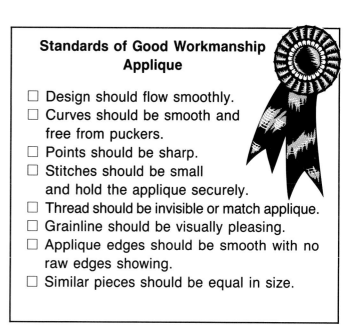

Standards of Good Workmanship
Applique

☐ Design should flow smoothly.
☐ Curves should be smooth and free from puckers.
☐ Points should be sharp.
☐ Stitches should be small and hold the applique securely.
☐ Thread should be invisible or match applique.
☐ Grainline should be visually pleasing.
☐ Applique edges should be smooth with no raw edges showing.
☐ Similar pieces should be equal in size.

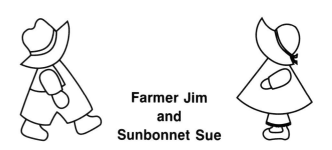

**Farmer Jim
and
Sunbonnet Sue**

Sunbonnet Sue and Farmer Jim are examples of applique popular at the turn of the century. The large hats predominate thus eliminating the need for facial features. These faceless children can engage in a wide range of activities just by slightly changing the position of the body and adding accessories.

The Farmer Jim pattern was developed by my friend, the late Pat Newkirk, for her son Jim when he was young.

When used in pairs, it is suggested that the figures be of equal size, face each other and be similarly placed on the foundation.

Templates

Templates for applique *do not contain* seam allowance.

Templates for applique will be cut from tagboard and also serve as *pressing templates* to assure a sharp edge.

☐ Templates do not include seam allowance.

☐ Seam allowance will be added during cutting by "eyeballing" the ¼″ seam allowance.

Large Applique Pieces

Large pieces are cut by placing template on right side of fabric. The right side of the template must be right side up. (Dress and hat for girl.) (Overalls, hat, shirt for boy.)

☐ Cut fabric design piece adding ¼″ seam allowance to fabric beyond template.

☐ Machine gather curved edges:
   • Place template on *wrong* side of fabric.
   • Pull up gathers.
   • Press fabric over template.
   • Use spray starch to hold edge.
   • Remove template.

☐ Press straight edges over template.
   • Clip into corners when necessary.
   • Sharply crease straight edges by pressing over template.
   • Use spray starch to hold edge.

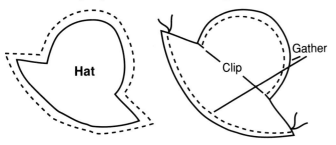

Small Applique Pieces
hands, sleeves, shoes, pantaloons

Small pieces are cut double. Cutting the small pieces double and turning them after the edge has been sewn gives a smooth edge even if you have ten thumbs.

☐ Cut pieces double, adding ¼″ seam allowance.

☐ Sew right sides together.

☐ Leave one side unsewn if it is to be covered by another piece.

☐ Trim seam to ⅛″.

☐ Turn piece right side out taking care to maintain shape.

☐ Use point turner to smooth edges.

☐ Press well rolling seam to back.

☐ Trim away back fabric, if desired.

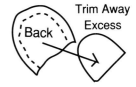

☐ If a piece is sewn on all sides and has no opening, slit back to turn.

Note: Applique sock to one shoe before finishing shoe for little girl.

To Finish Block:

☐ Make quilt sandwich: backing, batting, 13″ foundation.

☐ Center and lay out applique pieces on foundation.

☐ Plan logical sewing order.

☐ Pin or use glue stick to hold pieces in place while sewing.

☐ Stitch
   • use blind hem stitch or sew on very edge of applique
   • 12 to 16 stitches per inch
   • use invisible thread or thread to match applique.

☐ Quilt scenic background lines, if desired.

Embellish with embroidery stitches, laces, machine stitching, buttons, bows or ribbons, found objects.

Lisa Hanson made these blocks for her quilt. She is the new Mom pushing her baby. Her husband, David, operates the video camera.

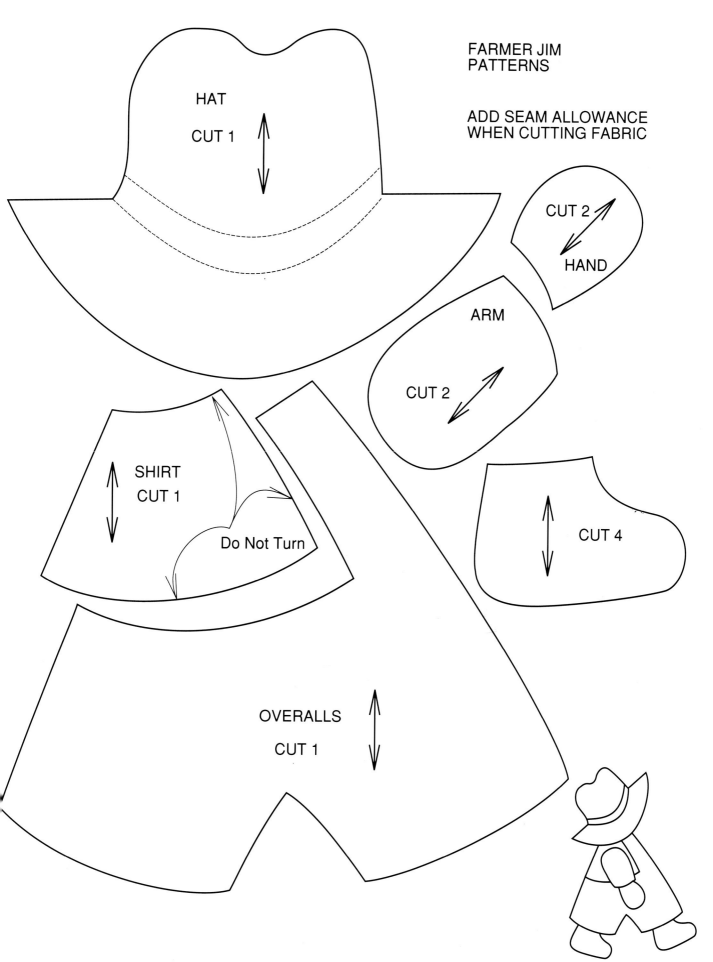

FARMER JIM
PATTERNS

ADD SEAM ALLOWANCE
WHEN CUTTING FABRIC

HAT
CUT 1

CUT 2
HAND

ARM
CUT 2

SHIRT
CUT 1

Do Not Turn

CUT 4

OVERALLS
CUT 1

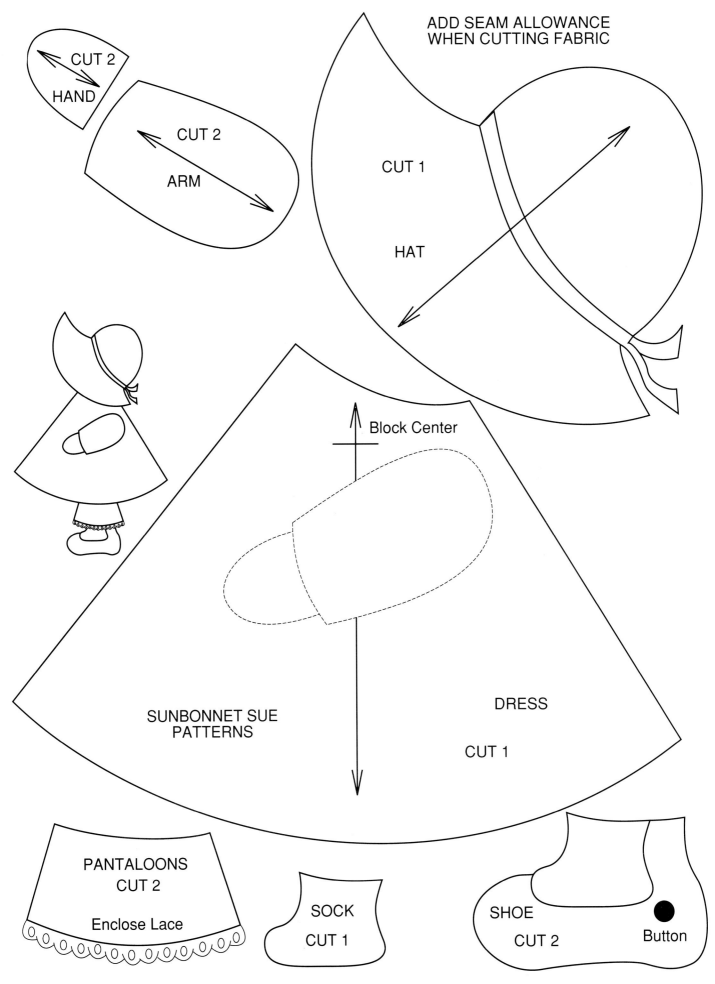

CUT 2
HAND

CUT 2
ARM

ADD SEAM ALLOWANCE
WHEN CUTTING FABRIC

CUT 1

HAT

Block Center

SUNBONNET SUE
PATTERNS

DRESS

CUT 1

PANTALOONS
CUT 2

Enclose Lace

SOCK
CUT 1

SHOE
CUT 2

Button

82

Pieced Picture Blocks

Pieced picture blocks are geometric. They can be decorated and trimmed with appliqued bushes and other details. A little pre-planning will allow you to include some of the appliqued edges in the seam allowances between the pieces of the block.

House On A Hill

Piece Your House! It may look like the traditional block or it could be a condominium or town house. Draft your own pattern or follow this one.

Personalize. House numbers, customized bushes and shutters add meaning. Lace

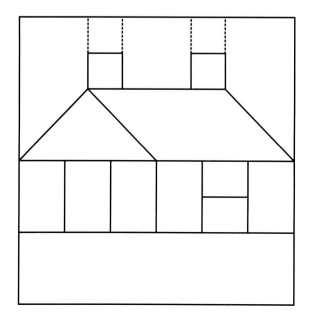

Note: Yellow windows make a cheery night house.

around gable and roof line works well and will fill in if roof doesn't exactly meet house.

Search for special fabrics that will work for you.

Pattern Drafting:
☐ Draft an irregular 4 patch.
☐ Divide 12″ square horizontally into quarters.

Lower section can be customized with a sidewalk, garden path or shadow if you desire.

The house and sky will be divided into 6 equal sections. The door and side sections are the same. One of those sections is divided for window and chimney template.

Add a gable, roof and small triangle.

Use 4 patch templates for square and triangle.

Seam allowance will be added to all pieces.

☐ Piece block in rows. Curtains can be sewn in the seam line.

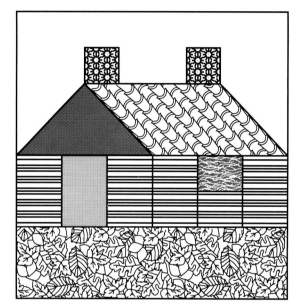

The Sailboat

Templates:
☐ Use 4 Patch templates.
☐ Water can be cut in one piece. (3½″ x 12½″)

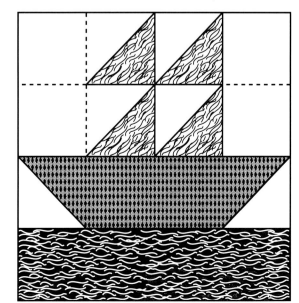

- ☐ Boat can also be cut in one piece.
  - Cut boat (3½ x 12½").
  - Place sky triangle on boat.
  - Pin in place and re-check position.
  - Sew.
  - Cut away excess "boat."
  - Press sky in position.

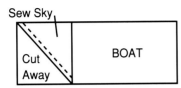

Special Touches:
- ☐ Lace can be inserted to resemble ocean foam.
- ☐ Quilt waves, wind, motion, birds and fish.

Airplane

Use templates given.
Piece on the diagonal.
A cloud or star fabric works well for background.
"Children" of all ages love this block.

Original Designs

Vacation memories can be captured and included in a quilt. Designing and drafting your own patterns from postcards or photographs is personally meaningful and unique.

Black Barn represents a composite of design elements found in black barns photographed in Kentucky.

Creating Designs

- ☐ Keep design simple.
  - Details can be added later.
  - Quilting will also strengthen design.
- ☐ Work on ¼" graph paper.
- ☐ Draw a small grid.
- ☐ Pencil in your main structure lines.
- ☐ If that grid does not work, try again on a different grid.
- ☐ Try again, if not satisfied.
- ☐ Refine design.
- ☐ Is piecing practical?
- ☐ Redesign if necessary.
- ☐ Make templates and block.

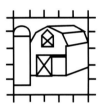

Black Barn

- ☐ Choose colors of your choice.
- ☐ String quilt fabric for barn, if desired.
- ☐ Cut barn pieces.
- ☐ Use double fold ¼" bias tape to applique barn door details.
- ☐ Use clam shell for top of silo.

Roseville Bridge – 1910

This block was designed from a vacation post card picturing the bridge that crosses Big Raccoon Creek at Coxville, Indiana. The bridge was built in 1910 and is 263' long and 16' wide.

☐ Piece inside of bridge:
  • Join 4 inside bridge pieces to end of bridge, matching pattern dots.

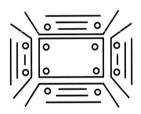

  • Sew to dots, leaving seam allowance free.
  • Join inside bridge seams.
☐ Replace upper corners of inner bridge with small triangles, if desired.
☐ This is a combination block using both a 4 Patch and a 9 Patch Grid.

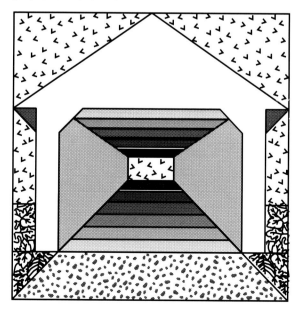

The Time Capsule or Crazy Patch

The Time Capsule is the contemporary Crazy Patch. Here is another chance for you to "leave a note." What were the major events of the year for you? Did you get a new car, move to a new home, attend a wedding? Stitch a word or two hidden among the scrap fabrics of the Time Capsule. What might seem silly as you stitch will become treasured in just a short time.

The Time Capsule is an original design as there is no pattern. You will be sewing down bits and pieces of fabric and other special laces or even fabric photographs to a foundation.

Your block may be making a final statement about your quilt.

This could be your signature block.

Time Capsule Directions

☐ Use a 15" backing and batting foundation.
☐ Sew clam shell scraps, laces, fabrics, photos directly to batting:
  • press edges under and applique
                    and/or
  • use sew and turn method from string quilting technique.
☐ Quilt using decorative stitches.
☐ Trim to 12½".

Photographs In Quilts

One more way to personalize a quilt is through the use of photographs. They can be made into a block design or incorporated into the Time Capsule. Why not include your photo along with your signature and date?

I have run across several methods of transferring pictures to quilts. I have chosen three methods which render three different types of reproduction. All are simple, safe, inexpensive and washable.

"Antique Look" Photographs

When a soft, delicate photographic image is desired, a direct color photocopy can be used. The results will be slightly muted often with a greenish tint. These pictures present an "Antique Look." This type of photo transfer works well in light colored or pastel quilts.

Directions:

Take a color photograph to a color photocopying center. Request an ordinary color photocopy. It will be printed on an 8½" x 11" piece of paper. Generally the copy center does not know what you are talking about when you tell them you will be transferring the picture to fabric. Don't worry.

By previously taping "a bunch" of photos to a piece of typing paper, you will have the picture you desire, plus extras to use for trial and error.

Directions:
- ☐ Select white cotton or muslin fabric.
- ☐ Place fabric on firm ironing board.
- ☐ Place photocopy upside down on fabric.
- ☐ Iron one minute with very hot iron, taking care not to scorch fabric.
- ☐ Lift one corner to check image.
- ☐ Image will be reversed and permanent.

Bright and Shiny Quilt Photos

Color photocopies can be transferred to fabric in another method. The initial process of having a photocopy made is the same as in the "Antique Process."

The photocopy is then transferred to a Iron-on Film which in turn is ironed onto a light colored fabric. The image is sharp, clear and permanently fused to the quilt fabric. The image is not reversed.

The surface remains shiny and the colors bright. The image is damaged by touching it with an iron, however. This type of reproduction fits in well with bright, strong colored quilts.

The iron-on film comes with complete and simple directions. It can be found in photographic or craft supply stores under various trade names.

Please see Supply List for supplier.

Muted Images on Fabric

Another method of transferring photographs to fabric is done with a special type of copy machine. The one used in the Christmas quilt is a Sharp CX 5000S. The picture is transferred directly from the original photograph to a plastic film. A commercial heat press is used to transfer the image to fabric.

This process gives a print that fits in well with slightly muted quilt fabrics. The image is well defined and not reversed. The original photograph is not harmed.

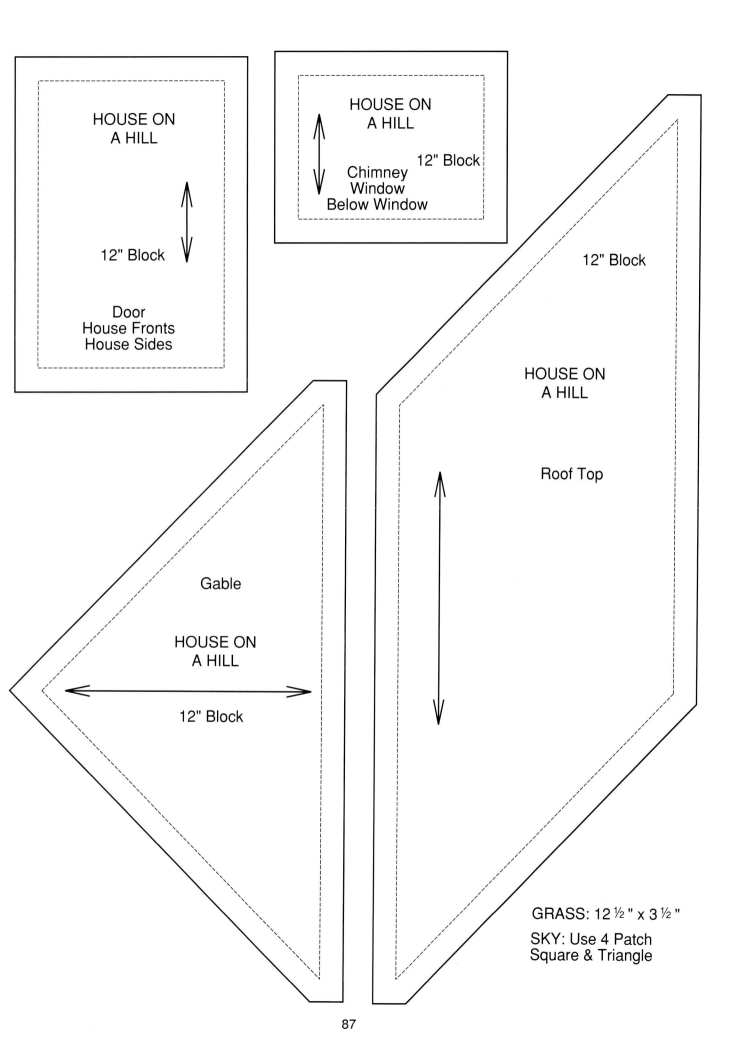

HOUSE ON
A HILL

12" Block

Door
House Fronts
House Sides

HOUSE ON
A HILL

Chimney
Window
Below Window

12" Block

12" Block

HOUSE ON
A HILL

Roof Top

Gable

HOUSE ON
A HILL

12" Block

GRASS: 12 ½ " x 3 ½ "

SKY: Use 4 Patch
Square & Triangle

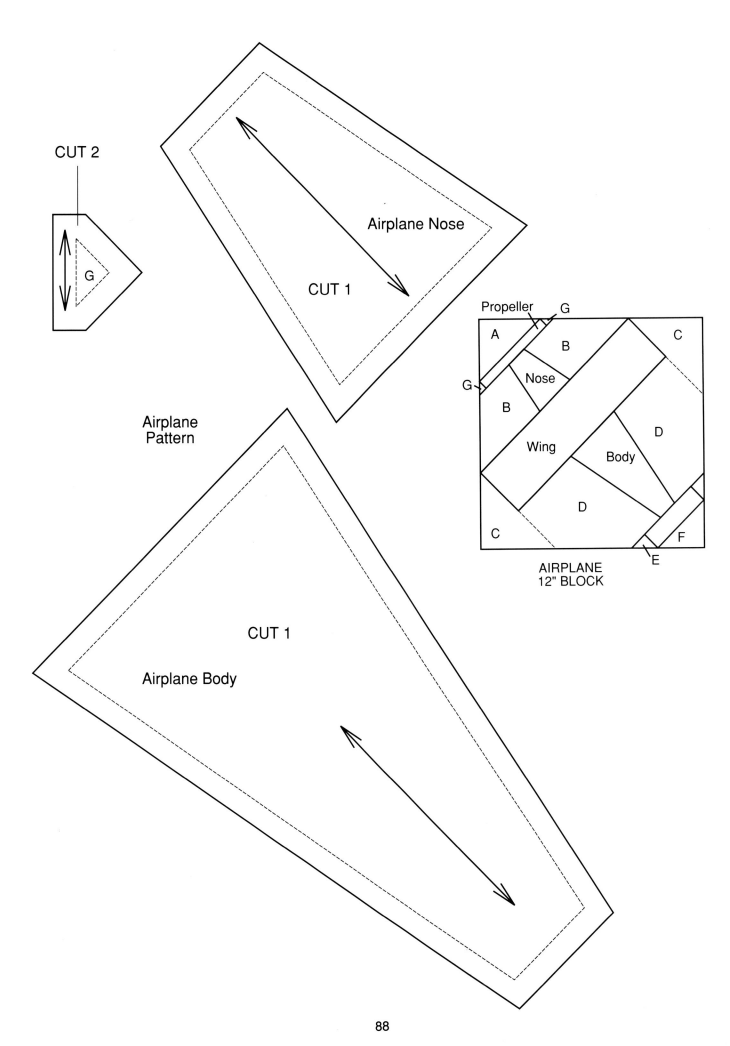

CUT 2

Airplane Nose

CUT 1

G

Propeller

G

A

B

G

Nose

B

C

Wing

D

Body

Airplane
Pattern

CUT 1

Airplane Body

D

C

E

F

AIRPLANE
12" BLOCK

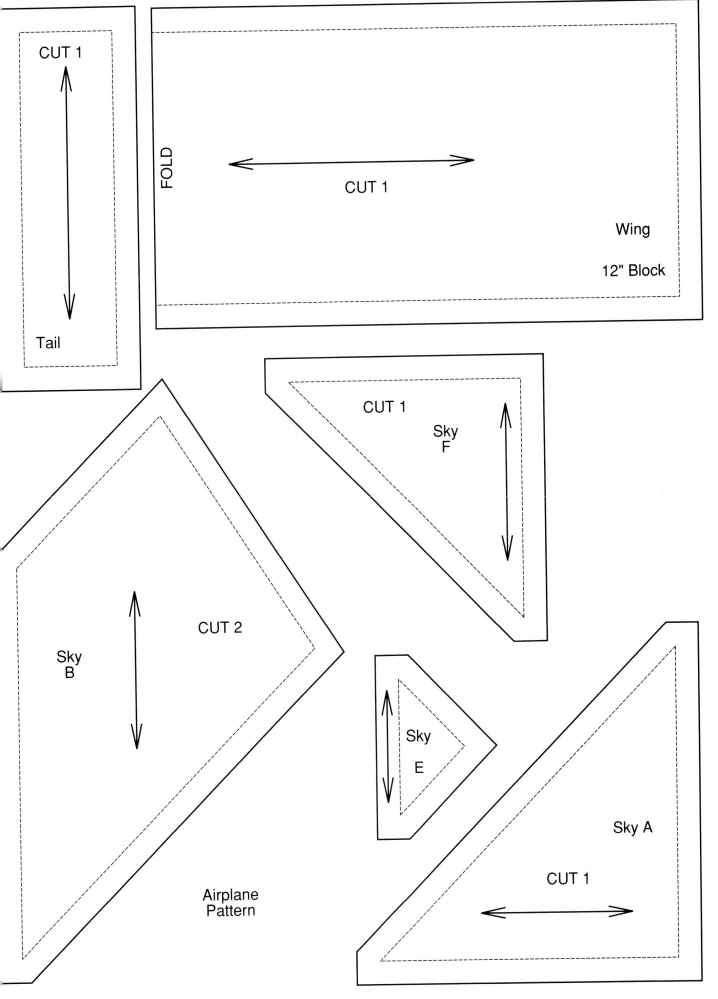

CUT 1

Tail

FOLD

CUT 1

Wing

12" Block

CUT 1

Sky
F

CUT 2

Sky
B

Sky
E

Sky A

CUT 1

Airplane
Pattern

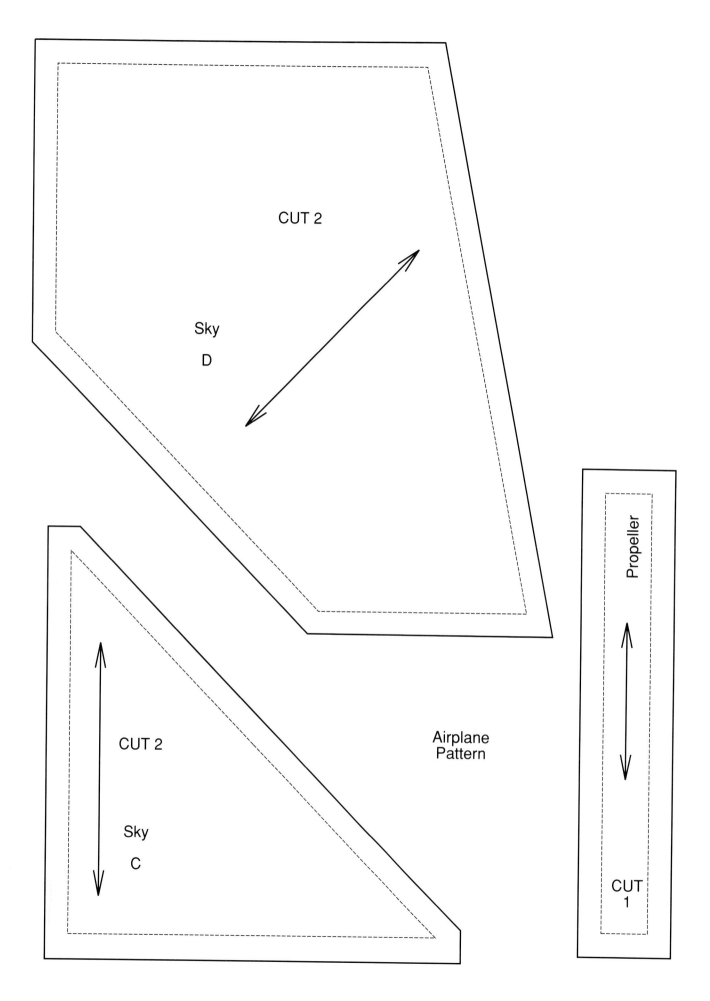

CUT 2

Sky

D

CUT 2

Sky

C

Propeller

CUT
1

Airplane
Pattern

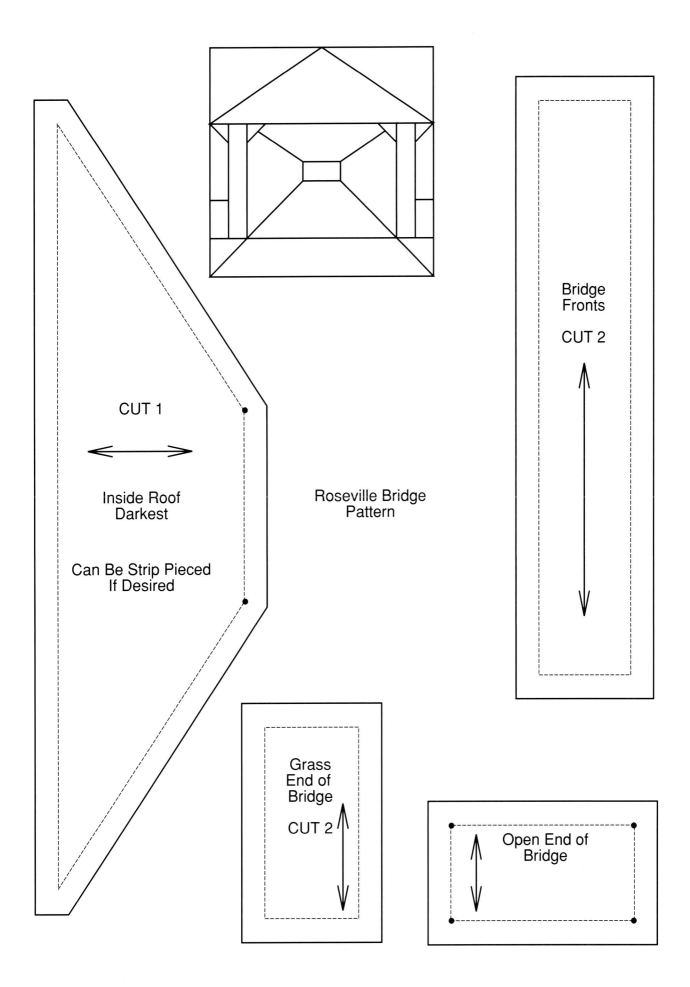

CUT 1

Inside Roof
Darkest

Can Be Strip Pieced
If Desired

Roseville Bridge
Pattern

Bridge
Fronts

CUT 2

Grass
End of
Bridge

CUT 2

Open End of
Bridge

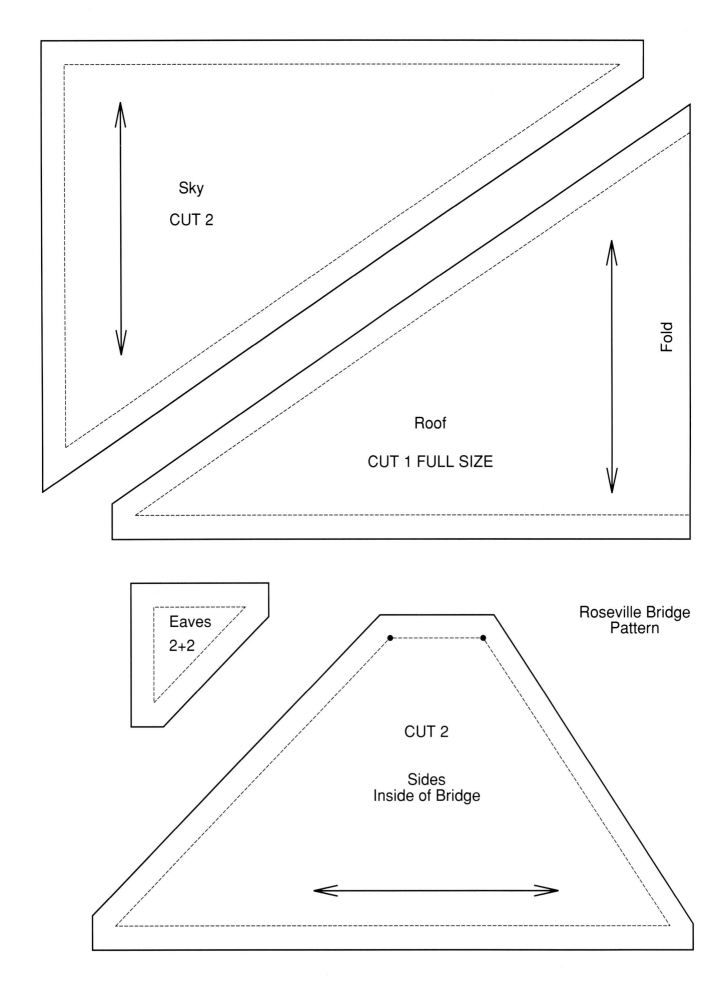

Sky

CUT 2

Fold

Roof

CUT 1 FULL SIZE

Eaves
2+2

Roseville Bridge
Pattern

CUT 2

Sides
Inside of Bridge

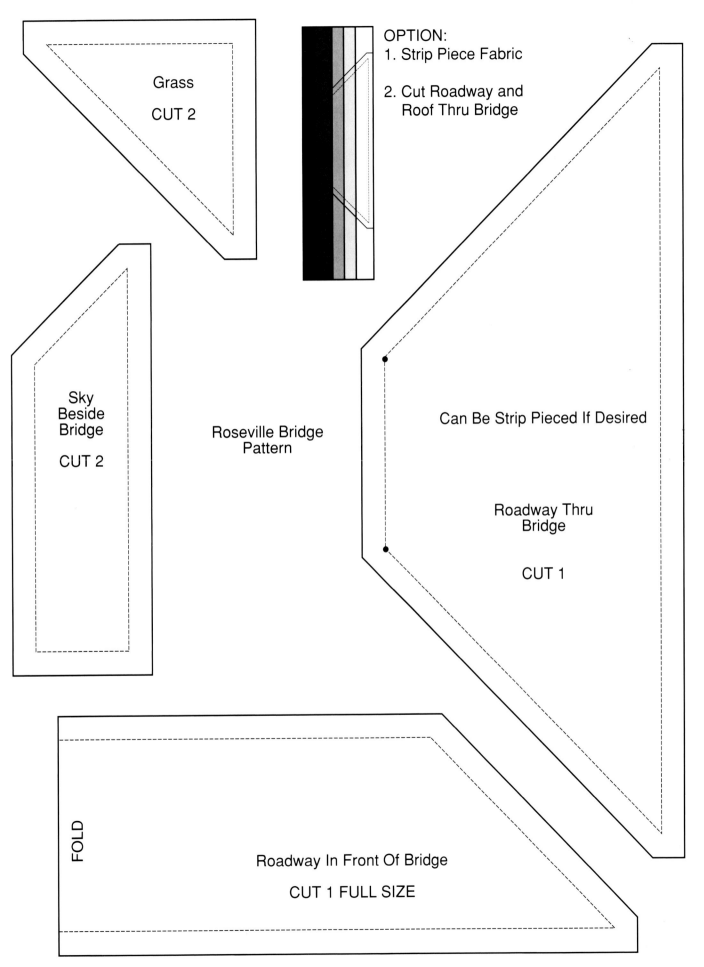

Grass
CUT 2

OPTION:
1. Strip Piece Fabric

2. Cut Roadway and
   Roof Thru Bridge

Sky
Beside
Bridge

CUT 2

Roseville Bridge
Pattern

Can Be Strip Pieced If Desired

Roadway Thru
Bridge

CUT 1

FOLD

Roadway In Front Of Bridge

CUT 1 FULL SIZE

Lesson Seven
Arranging the Blocks And Sashing

Sizing the Blocks
Arranging the Blocks
Choosing the Sashing Fabric

Mock String Sashing
Joining the Blocks

The blocks are finished, and it is time to make a quilt out of your Objects d'Art.

The finishing steps of joining the quilt blocks are as important as the making of the blocks. The process is more mathematical than the creative experiences you have had with the blocks. The finishing will go quickly when you understand the process and importance of each step.

Please take time to read through these last two chapters to get an overview of the finishing process. Understand the importance of blocks that are an equal size and why measurements should be accurate, written down and used as a reference as you work.

For this last stage of quiltmaking, you may choose to move your sewing machine to a large table or extend your sewing area with the addition of a card table or two.

Goal:
- ☐ Trim the blocks to a uniform size.
- ☐ Arrange the blocks attractively.
- ☐ Select the perfect sashing fabric.
- ☐ Make ''between'' sashing.
- ☐ Join blocks into vertical rows.

Lou Cole and her quilt in vertical rows.

Sizing The Blocks

Sizing The Blocks: Theoretically all of the finished blocks should measure a square 12½". Quilting, however, tends to shrink the blocks, and they may measure 12¼" or even less. There is no problem if all the blocks are the same size. However, blocks that are various sizes will not fit together well and the rows of blocks will wobble.

The goal is to have all blocks trimmed to the same size without cutting off the points of the design. The rotary cutter is the preferred trimming tool.

If a block is small by ¼" or more, it should be brought up to size by adding a small matching strip of fabric on one or more sides or just in the skimpy area. Attempting to stretch the block to fit into the quilt by using a narrow seam allowance will only lead to disaster.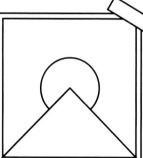

On occasion a strip frame will have to be placed on all four sides.

It is easy to bring a block up to size with the addition of a small border strip matching one of the colors in the block.

If a block is just *slightly* too large, *do not trim it* if trimming would affect the design points. A small amount of ease can be worked into a quilt.

Arranging The Quilt Blocks

The final placement of the blocks in the quilt will be determined by visual weight, color, color value and design.

The solid blocks, Log Cabin, String Quilting, Crazy Patch and Clam Shell appear to be visually heavier than the other designs. Placing them in the orners, over the pillow area or in the center of the quilt will distribute the weight.

The colors should be placed to present a coordinated and blending palate. Zinger fabrics should be well distributed throughout the quilt.

The curved blocks, Moon Over The Mountain, Drunkard's Path, Dresden Plate, Granny's Fan and Clam Shell should be alternated with the straight line designs for balance and flow.

Blocks should be arranged to maintain a *focus* in the center of the quilt. The applique boy and girl would make a nice center pair. If you have five rows across, the boy and girl can be separated by House on a Hill or Clam Shell.

Use the strong diagonal lines of Diagonal String and Jacob's Ladder to lead the eye into the center of the quilt.

Study Your Quilt Blocks

☐ Pin the blocks up for viewing on a wall, curtains or pin them to a sheet.
☐ Study the arrangement under different lighting and at different times of the night and day.
☐ Ask the opinion of a friend.
☐ Ask the opinion of a child and his or her friend.
☐ Take a picture of the hanging blocks for evaluation.
☐ Row two may be tucked under the pillow so don't place your favorite block there.
☐ When you are satisfied with your arrangement, label each block to keep them in order.

Sashing

The sashing unifies the quilt and establishes the color of the quilt. A quilt with blue sashing is usually thought of as THE BLUE QUILT, even if the blocks are predominantly tan and rust.

Sashing can spark a dull quilt or quiet a wild one. Sashing is chosen after the completion of the blocks.

Choosing the Sashing

Select:
☐ A quality fabric.
☐ Avoid plaids or stripes as they will not work well with the sashing method used for this quilt.

Take several of the completed blocks to the store when choosing the sashing fabric. Consider several different colors and values for sashing possibilities. Select the fabric that shows off the blocks to their best advantage.

Suggestions:

☐ A busy floral print adds charm and a country feeling to this IRIS quilt by Kathy Samone. The stenciled corner stones carry out the color scheme which is based on the iris.

☐ The black fabrics contrasted with the light blue in the sashing and corner stones adds a dramatic note to this quilt by Gertrude Braan.

☐ Pastel blocks maintain their "confection like" beauty when sashed by a light fabric. Quilt by Pam Junge.

☐ Dark sashing underscores the richness of t fabrics used in the blocks by Gerry Smith.

☐ A neutral sashing quietly frames the quilt bloc Note the three cats chasing about the border this quilt by Peggy Simon.

Sashing is a personal choice. The blocks in these two quilts are similar in value. The sashing changes the mood of the blocks.

ASIAN DELIGHTS by author.
First Place, NQA show, 1989.

Mock String Sashing

Mock string sashing rapidly transforms the sampler blocks into an heirloom quilt. The mock string quilting is created by folding the front sashing strip in half lengthwise and stitching ¼″ from the fold, forming an enclosed tuck.

The sashing will be stitched and simultaneously quilted in long strips. The first strips will be cut into short strips the exact width of the blocks. These short pieces are called *betweens* and will be sewn *between two blocks*, joining the blocks into vertical rows.

The simplicity of this markless finish compliments the busy designs in a SAMPLER quilt.

☐ Sew with evenfeed foot.

Since you will be sewing and quilting long strips, there is a tendency for the fabric to pull up slightly. The evenfeed foot will allow you to sew a three yard strip of fabric without distortion.

☐ Please refer to Layout/Cutting (Appendix).

Cutting (tearing) diagrams are suggested for the sashing. You will have identical fabric yardages for the front and the back sashing. Each front sashing piece will have a corresponding back sashing piece, and a piece of batting.

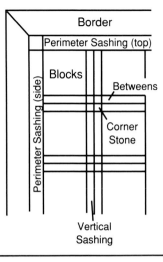

Make a diagram of your quilt and keep a Figures Chart:
☐ Draw squares to represent blocks.
☐ Add sashing (and border, if any).
☐ Finished block size _____.
☐ Quilt length_____.
☐ Quilt width _____.
☐ Border length _____.
☐ Border width _____.

Make notations on the chart as you progress. Quilt finishing does involve simple but accurate calculations. Check and double check your figures as you cut sashing and borders.

Sashing Preparation:

☐ Tear or cut all front and back sashing strips, 5″.
☐ Cut batting strips, 4+″.
☐ Label cut sashing strips:
  • Betweens – front
  • Betweens – back
  • Vertical Strips – front
  • Vertical Strips – back
  • Perimeter Sashing – front
  • Perimeter Sashing – back
Optional:
  • Borders – front
  • Borders – back

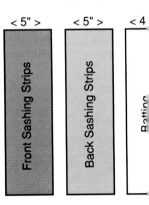

Front Sashing

- ☐ The finished width of the sashing will be 4″.
  One extra inch is allowed for seam allowances and the Mock String Tuck.
- ☐ Carefully iron front sashing strips in half lengthwise, right sides together.

The Betweens

- ☐ Making a sashing sandwich – from which to cut betweens.
  a. Backing – wrong side up
  b. Batting
  c. Folded top sashing (folded edge will extend ¼″ beyond center.
  Hint: Put a pin at Batting Center.
  Place a pin ¼″ from fold on front sashing strip.

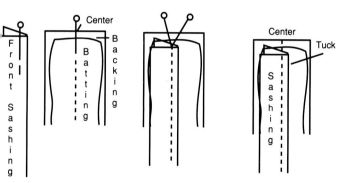

Lay front sashing on batting sandwich, aligning pins. The quarter inch fold will extend ¼″ to the right of center.
- ☐ Sew center quilting line:
  Right side of even feed foot will run along fold.
- ☐ Sew entire length of strip, needle stitching ¼″ from fold line.
- ☐ Maintain a straight stitching line.
- ☐ The ¼″ fold "tucks out" ½″ of fabric.
- ☐ Open up sashing strip and press front sashing lightly.
- ☐ Turn strip and press backing side.

Additional Quilting

Additional rows of quilting can be added 1″ on either side of first stitching line, if desired.
- ☐ Mark quilting lines by laying straight rows of ¾″ masking tape along center stitching line.
- ☐ Guide evenfeed foot next to tape and quilt using matching thread.

  or
- ☐ Use marking pen. Mark lines 1″ from center mock stitching line. Quilt.

Cutting The Betweens
- ☐ Cut designated strips into betweens.
  • Cut them into sections the width of your blocks.
- ☐ Be exact! All betweens will be the same size.

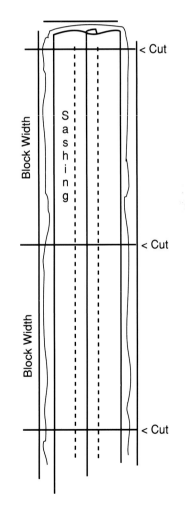

The sashing process may sound complicated, but after the first strip you will marvel at how easy it is.

Shrinkage Factor

Note: If an even-feed foot is not being used to quilt sashing strips, there may be some "shrinkage" as the long strips are sewn. While this is not a problem with the BETWEENS as they will be cut after being sewn, it could be a problem when using corner stones in the vertical sashings.

To avoid problems, calculate a "Shrinkage Factor."

☐ Before quilting, mark off a 36″ section on stripping.
☐ Quilt strip.
☐ Remeasure original 36″ section.
☐ Calculate shrinkage per yard.
☐ Calculate shrinkage per 12 inches by dividing by 3.

Joining Blocks

Front:
☐ With right sides together, join lower edge of block to between, sewing through:
- All layers of block.
- Front sashing and batting.
- Do not catch in the back of between.

Block
Front

☐ Continue adding blocks in vertical rows.

☐ "Slightly larger" blocks will be eased into size of between.

| 1 |
| 2 |
| 3 |
| 4 |
| 5 |

To finish back:
☐ Fold under the seam allowance on back of between.
☐ Place folded edge along stitching line.
☐ Pin in place.
☐ Sew by hand with small, secure blind hem stitch.

Block
Back

Block
Back

or

Machine blind hem stitch (like putting in a skirt hem)

- 30 stitches per inch
- Small jump over stitch
- Use thread to match back.

☐ Fold strip so block back is on top, between is under block.

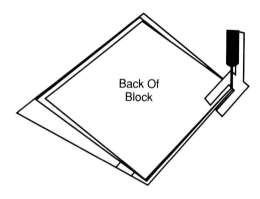
Back Of Block

- Sew on wrong side of turned-under seam allowance with blind hem stitch.
- Zig-Zag stitch will catch block.
☐ Join all blocks into long rows.
☐ Measure long block strip and record measurement on quilt diagram.

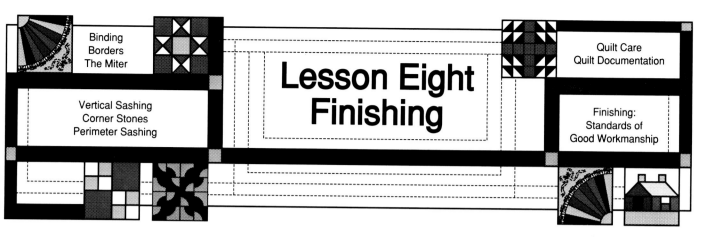

Lesson Eight
Finishing

Binding
Borders
The Miter

Vertical Sashing
Corner Stones
Perimeter Sashing

Quilt Care
Quilt Documentation

Finishing:
Standards of
Good Workmanship

The thrill of a finished quilt is at hand! The final finishing steps are as easy to understand and accomplish as the initial steps of sewing the betweens. The only difference is in the size of the quilt sections.

Goal: To complete your prize winning quilt

Skills: Vertical Sashing
   Perimeter Sashing
   Borders
   Miters

Vertical Sashing

Vertical sashing will join the completed rows of blocks. It can be totally the same color as the betweens or corner stones may be added.

Corner Stones

Corner stones are the optional colorful squares located at the intersection of the horizontal and vertical sashings. They help to align the blocks horizontally

and add a spot of accent color to the quilt front.

Corner stones are pieced into the long sashing strip before the strip is quilted.

Sashing With Corner Stones

Cut sashing strips into pieces the size of quilted blocks plus an allownce for shrinkage if necessary. (See Shrinkage Factor on page 100.)

☐ Cut corner stones 5″ wide by 4½″.
☐ Join sashing to small squares. (5 sashing pieces – 4 small squares per strip)
☐ Fold and iron strip in half length-wise.
☐ Quilt vertical strip to match betweens.

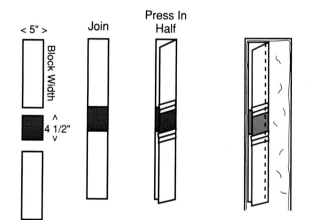

Joining Rows Together

☐ Sewing order:
   • Sew row one to row two
   • Sew row three to row four
   • Join sections one to two
   • Add perimeter sashing
☐ Position vertical strip on inside edge of first row of blocks, right sides together.
☐ Carefully match corner stone seam lines with between seam lines.
☐ Sew sashing to row of blocks.

- ☐ Trim out any excess batting.
- ☐ Add second row of blocks to other side of vertical sashing.
- ☐ Repeat with rows 3 and 4.
- ☐ Join both sections with last vertical strip.

Note: After quilt has been assembled, horizontal quilting lines can be added to corner stones, if desired. This involves shoving a lot of bulk under the machine and is not really necessary.

Vertical Strips Without Corner Stones

The decision to use corner stones is strictly arbitrary. They do help to align the blocks in straight horizontal rows.

If they are not used, the same benefit can be achieved by marking the vertical strip with a temporary but precise line as a reference for aligning vertical strip to rows of blocks.

- ☐ Assemble vertical sashing strip.
- ☐ Quilt strip.
- ☐ Mark intersections on vertical strip.
- ☐ Compare all marked strips to make sure markings are identical and accurate.

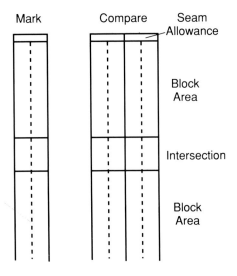

Join Sashing To Rows Of Blocks:

- ☐ Position strip on row of blocks.
- ☐ Align markings with betweens.
- ☐ Sew sashing to row of blocks.
- ☐ Trim out any excess batting.
- ☐ Finish back.

Perimeter Sashing

If no borders are to be included on the quilt, the perimeter sashing will frame and finish the quilt. The outside edge of the sashing can be finished before it is applied to the quilt thus eliminating an additional binding.

If corner stones have been used in the quilt, they can also be used in the perimeter sashing or eliminated entirely.

Finished Side Sashing

This sashing strip will look like the other sashing strips with the exception of the finished outside edge.
- ☐ Layer front and back sashing, right sides together, batting on bottom.

   (Front strip has been pressed in half but is now opened up so only one edge is caught in outside seam line.)
- ☐ Sew outside edge with ¼″ seam.

- ☐ Turn sashing, right sides out, enclosing batting.
- ☐ Establish attractive outside edge by rolling seamline slightly to the back and pinning frequently to maintain edge.
- ☐ Fold strip into position and quilt ¼″ from fold.
- ☐ Gently press sashing strips and outside edge, removing pins.

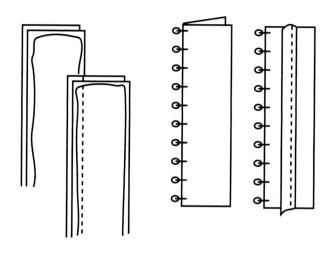

The finished outside strips are ready to be applied to the quilt core. Measure quilt length again, this time through the center of the quilt. The side will be cut to this exact measurement to assure an edge that is smooth and straight. If the perimeter sashing is too short, the side will draw up. If the sashing is too long, it will ripple.

Apply Quilt Sides to Quilt Core:
- ☐ Quarter edge sashing: find mid-point, quarter and three/quarter divisions.
- ☐ Find corresponding reference points on quilt core.
- ☐ Match reference points. Pin.
- ☐ Stitch from mid-point to outside edges.

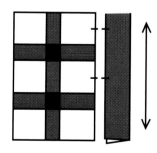

Finished Top and Bottom Sashing
The top and bottom perimeter sashing strips will be finished on the long side as well as the corners. Extra care must be taken to assure the proper sashing measurement after the outside edge has been sewn. The sashing tuck will be sewn twice.

- ☐ Measure the horizontal width of the quilt through the center of the quilt.
  - Use this measurement to determine final sashing width plus seam allowances.
  - Add a few extra inches for "insurance."
- ☐ Cut sashing strips desired width.

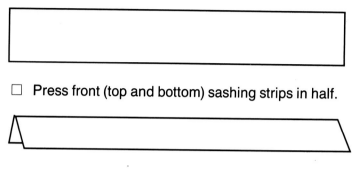

- ☐ Press front (top and bottom) sashing strips in half.

- ☐ Sew tuck, ¼″ from fold. Press tuck toward quilt seamline.

- ☐ Layer batting, back and tucked front (opened).
- ☐ Sew one corner and outside edge.

- ☐ Check strip width measurement to make sure that it did not shrink in sewing.
- ☐ Continue sewing last corner.

Finish Strip:
- ☐ Turn strip, right sides out.
- ☐ Pin to established final edge.
- ☐ Fold sashing out of the way to expose tuck.
- ☐ Sew tuck from end to end as far as possible, resewing over previous stitching line.

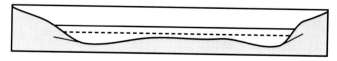

- ☐ Apply strip to quilt, right sides together.
- ☐ Finish back.

Optional Quilt Edge Finish

Binding

A narrow binding can be used to finish the edge of the quilt instead of the finished outside edge.

When binding is to be used, perimeter sashing or borders will be added to the quilt core in the same manner that the vertical sashing was added, marking and matching reference points.

Binding Size and Application

Before cutting all of the quilt binding, make yourself a mini-quilt sample. This will help you to understand the binding technique and determine the exact binding width for your quilt.

- ☐ Make a 5″ square quilt sandwich.
- ☐ Cut binding strip (either straight of grain or bias)
  - cut strip 1⅞″ wide
  - cut strip 30″ long
- ☐ Press strip in half, wrong sides together.

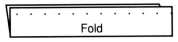
Fold

- ☐ Pin binding to right side of "quilt," matching raw edges. (Leave two inches of initial end free for later joining.)

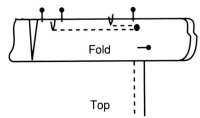
Fold

Top

- ☐ Sew with ¼″ seam allowance.
- ☐ Stop sewing ¼″ from end of "quilt" sandwich.
  - backstitch.
  - cut threads.
  - remove quilt from machine.
- ☐ Fold binding, forming a 45 degree angle.
  - finger press fold line.
  - pin in place.

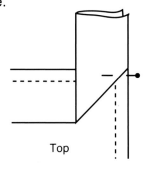
Top

- ☐ Fold binding in downward position:
  - place fold even with side one raw edges.
  - raw edges of binding will be even with side two.
- ☐ Sew from top of fold to next corner and repeat.

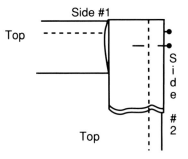
Side #1

Top

Top

Side #2

Joining Binding Ends With Bias "Seam"

- ☐ Allow 4″ for working room.
- ☐ CLIP fold line ½″ on right hand binding strip.
- ☐ Fold in ends forming bias end fold.
  - press or finger press fold
  - trim inside bulk
- ☐ Cut oncoming strip at similar 45 degree angle.
- ☐ Slip oncoming strip into folded end.
- ☐ Blind hem opening closed by hand when finishing rest of binding.

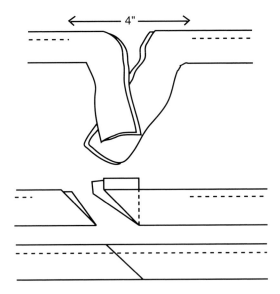
4″

Fold Binding To Back Of Quilt

- ☐ Slip stitch binding in place by hand with tight, invisible stitches, covering machine stitching lines.
- ☐ Fold miters in place at corners.
  - invisibly slip stitch meters with matching thread.

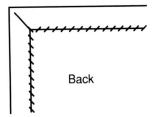
Back

Borders

If borders are to be added to the quilt to extend its size, the perimeter sashing would be added to the quilt first without finishing the outside edge.

Borders are meant to complement the quilt and act as a final frame. A 10″ border or less works very well both asthetically and yardage-wise. (Three yards has been allowed for border backing: four sides x 10″ border = 3 yards.)

The outside edge of the border can be prefinished or bound. The borders will be quilted and then applied to the quilt following the directions for perimeter sashing.

If large corner stones or pieced blocks are to be

used to finish the outside corners of the quilt, they will be added to the top and bottom strip before they are added to the quilt.

Striped Borders

A striped fabric generally makes a wonderful quilt border. It relates to the quilt if some of the fabric has already been pieced into the blocks. It also provides a markless quilting motif to follow.

In using a stripe, it is desirable to have all four corners be identical. This is not difficult as long as a little forethought is given during the cutting and planning stage.

The borders will have to be cut the length of the quilt plus extra inches for the mitered corners. (Two times the width of the borders plus seam allowances.) In the planning stage, cut your border strips even longer than needed to allow freedom in experimenting with the design.

Study your striped fabric design and find a starting point or center point of the design. Think of this spot as the design reference mark. If this mark is placed in the exact center of each quilt side, the four corners will be identical.

If a pleasing corner design is not achieved with your first layout, keep the design reference mark in the center of two opposing or opposite sides and try a different design mark for the other two borders. Again, the corners will all be identical. Play and plan with this a bit before you sew.

- ☐ Corner design elements should be identical.
  - • If design elements at midpoint of opposing borders are identical, the four corners will be identical.
  - • Try various mid-point designs to determine which design will be most attractive when stitched into the corner miter.
- ☐ Mitered borders require extra inches. The borders must be cut:
  - • the length of the quilt plus 2 times the border width plus seam allowances. Add 2″ for insurance.
  - • the width of the quilt plus 2 times the border width plus two seam allowances. Add 2″ for insurance.
- ☐ Assemble Borders:
  - • Layer backing & stripe, right sides together. Batting on bottom.
  - • Sew outside edge.
  - • Turn: establish edges with pins.
  - • Quilt strip only in quilt core area. Leave border overlap area unquilted.
- ☐ Apply Borders:
  - • Quarter quilt and borders.
  - • Position identical design motif on opposing mid-points.
  - • Match reference points on quilt and borders.
  - • Sew from mid-point to edge. Stop seam ¼″ from edge of quilt core.

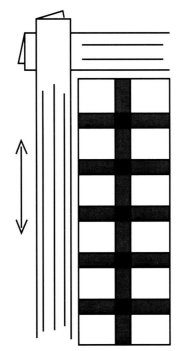

The Miter

- ☐ Work on a large, flat surface.
- ☐ Smooth side border up in continuing straight line.
- ☐ Trim excess from top of side border but leave ½″ seam allowance.
- ☐ Tuck seam allowance to inside.
- ☐ Smooth top border under side border.
- ☐ Trim excess from top border but leave ½″ seam allowance.
- ☐ Tuck seam allowance to inside.
- ☐ Fold top border into a 45° angle at corner, matching design element.
- ☐ Trim away excess fabric and batting.

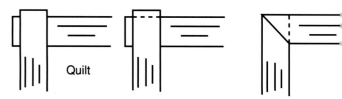

- ☐ With matching thread, hand sew miter with small, invisible stitches.
- ☐ Finish back with miter.

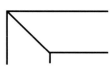

- ☐ Finish quilting corners.

Standards of Good Workmanship

Finishing

- ☐ Sashing strips should be even width.
- ☐ Sashing should not ripple, curve or pucker and should be joined to blocks without pleats or tucks.
- ☐ Corner stones should be perfectly matched to adjoining sashings.
- ☐ Borders should be smooth without ripples, curves or puckers.
- ☐ Piecing of a fabric in border should be symmetrical and unobtrusive.
- ☐ Border corners should be identically and exactly executed.
- ☐ Binding should be even and firmly filled with batting. Corners should be sewn, binding seams should be bias to eliminate bulk.
- ☐ Finishing stitches should be tight and apparently long lasting.

Hanging Sleeve

Your quilt may some day hang in a show or on a wall. Why not make a hanging sleeve now while the fabrics are at hand?

To make a finished four-inch hanging sleeve:

- [ ] Cut one long strip of fabric 9″ times the width of your quilt plus 2″ for turning under raw edges. OR Piece together fabrics from your quilt to make a strip the above size. This will give you a readily available fabric supply that could be used for repair in case of any quilt damage.
- [ ] Turn under short ends and stitch.
- [ ] Sew long sides, right sides together, forming a tube.
- [ ] Turn tube right sides out.
- [ ] Securely blind hem top and bottom edge of tube to quilt by hand.

Hooray! Shout!

Jump For Joy!

What a thrill to finish a quilt. Be sure to enter it in the county fair.

Kai Rim Park entered her quilt in the Montgomery Country Fair in Maryland and won first prize in the *First Quilt* category and Best of Show in the *Combined Hand and Machine* category.

Documentation

Each quilt is special to the maker. It is assumed that somewhere on the front of the quilt you have signed your name, city and date.

Each quilt has a story to tell. Even if there were no special theme to the initial pile of fabrics, there probably is some sort of a quilt-related tale to be told at the completion of the quilt. This should all be recorded. You may also wish to list the names of all the blocks so that others can share the pattern titles.

Documentation can be typed on a piece of light colored fabric and sewn to the back of the quilt. Typing on fabric is washable and permanent.

Hint: Fabric that has been ironed to a piece of freezer paper will roll through the typewriter with ease. Remove paper when finished.

Quilt Care

If this quilt has been made as a gift, include washing instructions and a bottle of washing detergent made especially for quilts. Suggest to the recipient that the quilt need not be washed often.

Vacuuming a quilt or airing it will remove surface dust.

The quilt may be washed in a home washing machine using the gentle cycle. Use warm or cold water. Remove immediately at the end of the washing cycle to avoid the possibility of one fabric fading or running onto another. Dry in the drier, but avoid over-drying.

PART THREE

The Making Of A Quilt Artist

Thinking More About Color
Fabric Dyeing
Adding Texture To Fabric And Quilts

The Making Of A Quilt Artist

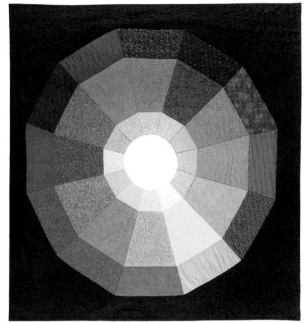

by Author

Thinking More About Color

The completion of the first quilt brings immense satisfaction and generally a desire to continue quiltmaking. The skills you have already acquired can be honed by experience and enriched by experimentation and study.

The color wheel and the color harmonies can be studied and analyzed. When you start discovering color chords in the sunset, in the spilled oil on the pavement, the TV commercials, and in the gumball machine at the local drug store – then you are truly becoming aware of color and color relationships. Your quilts will soon reflect this awakened sensitivity to the environment and its blending hues.

Developing A Color Confidence

After viewing a quilt show, one might conclude that every represented quiltmaker had been born with a wonderful awareness of color and an ability to put it all together. The hard fact is, that behind each quilt have gone many hours of deliberation and perhaps agony. Selected fabrics must be sorted, balanced, discarded and replaced before a color scheme is truly workable. This process of refinement requires observation, study and patience.

Fortunately there are some fundamental rules of color that can help to simplify the understanding and organization of color.

The Color Wheel

A color wheel visually illustrates the systematic relationship between colors. A knowledge and understanding of the 12 division color wheel helps to translate ideas for quilts into beautiful reality.

Color Vocabulary

Hue: the name of a color. Red is a hue or a color.
Value: the lightness or darkness of a hue or fabric. A value can be modified by adding white or black
  Tint: the amount of white in a hue or fabric.
  Shade: the amount of black in a hue or fabric.
Intensity: the brightness or dullness of a hue.
  High Intensity: brilliant, strong, saturated, maximum
  Low Intensity: muted, grayed, dull, muddy
  Tone: the amount of gray in a hue or fabric.
Warm Colors: red, orange, yellow.
Cool Colors: green, blue, violet.

Color Harmonies

Color, like music, has harmonious chords based on sequence and balance. These color chords act as guidelines for artists and quilters alike. By studying the sets of hues that are known to be visually pleasing, you may be able to add something to your quilts that will take them from the ordinary to the extraordinary.

A working knowledge of the color chords enables the quiltmaker to select fabrics with more ease and to stretch the limits of color harmony with creativeness and imagination.

Monochromatic

One color combined with various shades, tints and intensities of the same color or one color combined with black or white or neutrals. An example of a monochromatic quilt is found on page 111, AND IT RAINED FOR FORTY DAYS AND FORTY NIGHTS.

Analogous Harmonies

Touching colors on the color wheel.

An analogous color harmony uses touching colors to produce a blending, closely related color scheme. Interest is peaked by the addition of a small touch of color from across the color wheel.

MISTY MORNING, page 112, uses the cool combinations of blue, green and purple to convey the feeling of an early morning mist. Only a few touches of the hot pink break through the morning fog.

In choosing colors for this piece, I tried to imagine that every fabric chosen was seen through a mist. The various colors are then unified by the amount of "gray" in each piece.

Complementary Colors

A complementary color scheme is based on colors that are more or less opposite each other on the color wheel. (See Golden Memories of Christmas, page 113.) Red and green are complementary colors that work well. Blue and orange combinations are popular with artists and quilters. Yellow and violet are opposites but are not used in quilts as frequently in American culture.

A complementary color scheme gives the quiltmaker plenty of room to play with color. A wide color and value range can be incorporated in the quilt. The intensity, the amount of gray, should remain fairly constant.

To determine which fabrics would work best, take water color paints and mix the two complements together. All of the wonderful colors and neutrals that you produce with the paints can be translated into fabric and into an exciting quilt.

Fabric dyeing is another way to create fabrics for a complementary color scheme. The complementary colors are bridged producing a wonderful sweep of exciting and often surprising neutrals.

Triad (Equilateral)

A triad is a color harmony composed of three colors that are equadistant on the color wheel. (See Heritage, page 114.) To select a triad color scheme you would pick one color, skip three, pick one, skip three and pick one more. The color scheme, red, blue and yellow is probably the most popular triad used in quiltmaking. Blue is always a favorite color for quilts. The addition of red with a touch of yellow makes a very nice combination.

As with any color harmony, the neutrals of white, tan or gray can be used to extend the color range. Frequent use of the neutrals dilutes the color scheme.

Using a color harmony is an excellent guide for the quiltmaker in choosing fabrics. It should not hinder creativity, however. If you would like to add a bit of green or any other color to a red, blue and yellow triad,

you are certainly free to do so.

As a suggestion, use two of the colors in light, medium and dark values. The third color becomes the *spark* to ignite. Unify the color scheme by keeping the intensity fairly consistent.

Triad (Isosceles)

The isosceles triad also allows plenty of room for creative color expression. To select the colors for this triad, choose a pair of complementary colors. Use one of those chosen but eliminate the other. Select the two colors on either side of the eliminated color.

Blue, green and red-orange is an example of an isosceles triad. This is a wonderful color scheme! You can have blue for the water or sky, green for the grass and red-orange for accent.

SPRINGTIME SAMPLER, page 116, uses this color harmony. In this quilt, the corner stones have been stenciled with an oil stick stencil paint.

Other color harmonies that may work well for you:
Tetrad (square)
☐ 4 Equidistant colors
☐ Pick one, skip 2, pick one, skip 2, etc.
Tetrad (rectangular)
☐ Select opposite colors but do not use them.
☐ Use the two colors on either side of the above.

Hexad
☐ Use six colors
☐ Pick one, skip one
☐ Keep color values similar.
The Dance of the Sprites is an example of this color harmony executed in light value fabrics.

General Observations:
☐ Quiltmakers often confuse the terms fabrics and colors.
  • A monochromatic color scheme may have 12 fabrics but only one color. All the chosen fabrics can be shades or tints of the same color.
  • A triadic harmony could have 50 different fabrics but only 3 different colors.
☐ The number of different fabrics to be used in a project is proportionate to the size of the project.
  • A doll quilt or pillow needs only a few fabrics.
  • A wide range of fabrics adds depth and interest to a large quilt.
☐ Neutral colors (black, white, tan, gray) can be used to dilute and unify a harmony.

AND IT RAINED FOR FORTY DAYS AND FORTY NIGHTS by author.
From the collection of Frank and Dorothy Sullivan, Rockville, Maryland.

MISTY MORNING by author.

GOLDEN MEMORIES OF CHRISTMAS by author.
Winner: Best of Show, Houston Quilt Festival, 1988.

HERITAGE by author.
Winner from State of Maryland: We The Quilters Exhibition, 1987.

SUMMERTIME SAMPLER by author.
From the permanent quilt collection, American Quilter's Society, Paducah, KY.

SPRINGTIME SAMPLER by author.
Blue Ribbon Winner, Montgomery County Fair, Maryland, 1986.

Fabric Dyeing

Being able to dye fabrics in a wide range of shades and tints adds one more exciting aspect to the art of quiltmaking. Many quiltmakers and fiber artists are experimenting with fabric dyeing using Procion dyes. Procion dyes are fiber reactive. They react with the fabric (and water) to produce colors or hues which are wash-fast and light-fast.

Fabric dyeing is a "hands-on" learning experience that develops a more thorough understanding of color while producing an integrated palate of fabrics.

SPIRAL uses various shades of blue in a sequence to give the feeling of depth as the narrow staircase winds down to a mysterious black doorway.

SPIRAL STAIRCASE by author.
Collection of Christina O'Boyle.

THE WANG BUILDING, Bethesda, Maryland, by author, achieves its angular illusion from the eight graduated shades of brown and gray.

PAINT RAG by author.
Paint Rag uses a dyed blue sequence, a green sequence, and one purchased coordinating fabric.

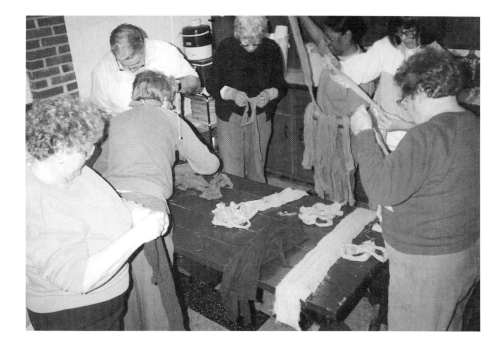

Desaturating A Color

Fabric stores carry such a wide selection of colored fabrics that it is rarely necessary to dye a piece of fabric to obtain a particular hue. However, a graduated series of a given color is difficult to find. This is the fun of fabric dyeing.

Fabric dyeing can produce fabrics in a sweep of colors. These color gradations add depth and highlights to a quilt.

Tints Of A Color are created by adding less and less dye to a series of dye pots. In dyeing, white is not added to the dye, but the amount of dye is reduced, desaturated, producing the lighter tints of fabric.

Shades are made by adding black to the dye (¼ t.).

Tones are made by adding brown to the dye (¼ t.).

Complementary Colors can be bridged creating neutral gray between the two complementary colors.

Fabrics:
- ☐ 100% cotton muslin, bleached or unbleached.
- ☐ Cottons appropriate for quilting. (Fabrics without perma-press finishes work best.)
- ☐ Fabrics should be washed in hot, soapy water before dyeing if they have any sizing or finish.
- ☐ Fabrics without finishes do not require prewashing.

Safety Basics:
- ☐ Powdered Procion dyes are toxic. Do not inhale.
- ☐ Dyeing utensils should not be used for cooking.
- ☐ Wear mask when mixing dye and rubber gloves at all times.

Equipment:
- ☐ 8 five gallon buckets
- ☐ Measuring spoons
- ☐ Timer (60 minutes)
- ☐ Stirrers (dowling works well)
- ☐ Pyrex measuring cups
- ☐ Dust mask
- ☐ Rubber gloves

Supplies:
- ☐ Procion dye
- ☐ Water softener if water is hard
- ☐ Salt – opens fabric fibers
- ☐ Soda ash or washing soda (carbonate of soda) – sets dye
- ☐ Water

Creating A Sweep Of Tints

Eight yards of fabric will be dyed in a progressive series of tints. The eight yards will be divided into eight one yard pieces, one yard for each bucket. The amount of dye required is based upon the total yardage to be dyed.

8 buckets x 1 yard = 8 yards of fabric to be dyed

Note: Calculations are also figured for dyeing 4 or 12 yards.

1 C = 16 Tbs.	1 Tbs. = 3 tsp.		3 yds. muslin = 1 lb.

Dye Requirements

Total Yds.	4 Yds.	8 Yds.	12 Yds.
Dye:			
Pale:	⅜ tsp.	¾ tsp.	1⅛ tsp.
Medium:	¾ tsp.	1½ tsp.	2¼ tsp.
Dark:	1½ tsp.	3 tsp.	4½ tsp.

These dye proportions are starting points. It takes less red than indicated. Red dye is very intense. On the contrary, it takes more yellow because the yellow dye is not as powerful. Fabric dyeing takes experimentation and record keeping.

Other Requirements For Each Bucket:			
Fabric:	½ yd.	1 yd.	1½ yd.
Water	1 gal.	2 gals.	3 gals.
Water Softener	2 tsp.	4 tsp.	6 tsp.
Salt	½ cup	1 cup	1½ cups
Soda (later)	2 Tbs.	4 Tbs.	8 Tbs.

Directions

- [ ] Fill buckets with warm water (100°)
- [ ] Add water softener to water if water may be hard
- [ ] Add salt (iodized or plain). Stir until dissolved
- [ ] Put on mask
- [ ] Mix dye

Dye will be worked into a paste with a small amount of warm water. Water will be added to make a 2 cup dye concentrate solution.

By using the water replacement method, half of the dye, 1 cup, will be added to the first pot. An equal amount of water will be replaced in the concentrate. As you proceed to the next pot, you will again be dividing the amount of dye in half and replacing that amount with water.

You will always have two cups of concentrate as you approach the next bucket or pot. There will be one cup of concentrate left to discard at the end.

Pot 1: 1 cup dye concentrate to dye pot. Replace with 1 cup of water.

Pot 2: Add 1 cup dye concentrate. Replace with 1 cup water. Continue . . .

- [ ] Add fabric
- [ ] Set timer for 30 minutes. Re-arrange and stir fabric in dye pot often
- [ ] Remove fabric temporarily
- [ ] Add soda dissolved in water
- [ ] Replace fabric
- [ ] Set timer for 1 hour
- [ ] Stir every 10 minutes
- [ ] Rinse fabrics
- [ ] Wash in washing machine, dry in dryer

Desaturation of Complementary Colors

This is a double desaturation using two complementary dye concentrates. Total amount of dye will be twice as strong as the single desaturation.

Working from left to right the pots will be desaturated with the first dye concentrate. No dye will be added to the last pot from this concentrate.

Mix up second concentrate.
Work from right to left!
Start adding concentrate with the far right pot. Do not add concentrate to far left pot.

First Dye Concentrate

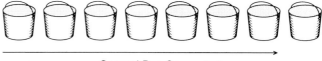

Second Dye Concentrate

Fabric Dyeing Record

Date _____   Total Amount of Fabric _____

Project _____   Number of Pots _____

Fabric _____   Fabric/Pot _____

Dyeing Friends _____

Pot #	Water Sftnr. Amt.	Amt. Salt	Formula Dye	Fabric Time In (30 min.)	Amt. Soda	Soda Time In (60 min.)	Swatches

Adding Textures . . . To Fabric Design

Quilting holds the three layers of the quilt together while giving dimension to the surface. Dimension can also be added to the quilt surface by actually adding texture to some of the fabric pieces before they are put into the quilt.

Fabrics can be manipulated in a great variety of ways and still remain supple enough to be used most successfully in the traditional quilting designs. This creates excitement and interest in contemporary quilts and keeps the art of quiltmaking alive and growing.

Pushing the limits of quiltmaking adds a touch of whimsy or light heartedness to a quilt. Creative texturing brings joy to the quiltmaker as well as the quilt viewer. It's fun. All it takes is a little imagination.

Adding texture to a quilt surface is not entirely new, however. Antique quilts have been known to have flowers that lift from the surface, ribbons that twist and three dimensional flowers made from rick rack. In her book on quilting, Averill Colby described "gathered patchwork . . . that had a certain popularity . . . during the middle of the nineteenth century."

Fabrics Manipulated

Fabrics can be manipulated to create a different look or texture. This is done before the design pieces are cut as the texturing changes the size and shape of the fabric. Once you start playing with fabrics in this manner you will think of more and more ways to change the looks of your fabrics.

Textured work should blend in with the theme of the quilt. It should not be heavy and over-powering. Fun and moderation should go hand in hand when creating textured fabrics.

Elastic Thread Fun

Elastic thread can be used to create a fabric that is deeply textured. Elastic thread is used in the bobbin. Fabric and batting (for depth) are stretched in a hoop. After stitching large circles about the size of a large pea on the surface of the fabric, the hoop is released. The fabric shrinks and puckers. The design pieces are then cut from the puckered fabric.

DRESDEN PLATE with elastic puckered center.

Supplies Needed:
  7″ spring hoop
  Elastic thread for bobbin
  Darning foot or darning spring
  Batting (optional)

Machine Setup:
  Drop or cover feed dogs
  Use darning foot or spring
  Elastic thread in bobbin

Stitch:
  Large circles
  Try other patterns also

Applications:
  Water
  Flowers
  Center of Dresden Plate
  Bushes or trees
  Pebbled walkways
  Added interest to any shape.

Elastic thread in the bobbin of the sewing machine can produce as many unique textures as can be imagined. Experiment by stitching different shapes. The process is one that requires only minimal practice and a sewing machine with feed dogs that can either be dropped or covered.

If batting is omitted, the elastic thread will draw up more creating a tighter, puckered fabric.

VIEW FROM HOME by author.

Snow and Sky: achieved by using the reverse sides of green and blue fabrics.
Angels In The Snow: stenciled and stitched.
Trees: machine stitched in gray thread.
Plant Leaves: sewn double, turned and stitched to wallhanging only through the center vein to give a three-
        dimensional plant.

SPRING GLORY by author.

Pink bushes: elastic thread in bobbin, no batting.
Green Bushes: crumpled and stitched fabric.
Sky: hand-dyed fabric.
Tree branches: bias branches, appliqued.
Tree Blossoms: variegated rayon thread, double needle stitching.
Wave: double needle stitching.

Crumples and Pleats

Crumpled fabric produces an irregular surface which works well in many designs.

GOD'S EYE Adaption

In the God's Eye block, crumpled fabric creates a nest for the ultra suede bird, while pieces of appliqued string add reality to the scene.

Crumples:

Fabric can be crumpled by tieing dampened yardage into a small ball. When dry, the fabric will be sharply creased and crumpled. To preserve the crumples, carefully place them on a piece of light weight scrap or stay fabric. Stitch crumples to stay fabric, hiding stitching underneath folds of the fabric. Maintain the wrinkled appearance of the fabric.

To Stitch Crumples:
- ☐ Lower feed dogs
- ☐ Use darning foot
- ☐ Hide stitching under raise wrinkles
- ☐ Extra embellishments can be stitched under the folds for added interest.

FOREST FLOOR is a wallhanging utilizing many textured effects. The background fabric is crumpled with small "twigs" stitched under a few of the raised wrinkles.

FOREST FLOOR by author

The small scattered leaves are sewn double, sli in the back and turned. The little flowers are yo-yo's gathered circles.

The large leaves are stuffed for added relief.

Pleats

The fabric for the little trees has been pleated by running it through a smocking machine. To secure the pleats before stitching into the block design, the pleated fabric was pressed onto a piece of freeze paper (shiney side up) for stabilization.

Small strips of smocked fabric can be included in string quilting.

GOLDEN MEMORIES

Gathered Strips

Long strips of fabric can be gathered up to be used in a wide variety of ways. Small gathered areas can add interest in a pieced block. String quilting can take on new interest with an occasional gathered strip. Whole borders can contain gathered strips.

In the WINTER'S COMFORT quilt, I wanted to use a particular light colored fabric in the border. However, I felt the fabric had a feel that was too delicate to hold such a dark border together. Thus, by gathering the dainty fabric it took on a stronger appearance which seemed to work well in the border.

Supply List:
Elastic thread, ruffler or gathering foot
Fabric strips cut desired width plus seam allowance

Machine Setup:
Elastic thread in bobbin
Regular presser foot
Feed dogs in normal position
Top tension may be altered (+ or −) to adjust gathering

If your machine has a gathering attachment or a foot that gathers, try those instead of the elastic thread. Choose the one that works best for you.

Procedure:
☐ Cut long strips desired width plus seam allowance.
☐ Gather flat material by running seam allowance under the presser foot:
  • regular thread in needle.
  • elastic thread in bobbin.
☐ Allow fabric to flow freely through machine.
☐ Gather both edges of fabric.
☐ Use as regular fabric.

Note: If gathered strip is to be used in a border, use a stay fabric to stabilize border.

Double Needle Ridges

Double and triple needles offer possibilities unlimited. The multiple needles are suspended from a single shank, each needle requiring a spool of thread. There is only one bobbin thread, and that tends to pull the top threads slightly to the back forming a ridge or a pin tuck on the fabric surface. The tighter the top tension, the sharper the pintuck.

The fabric in CHURN DASH was tucked with a 2 mm. double needle and then cut into shape for the design.

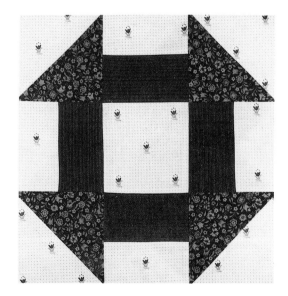

Machine Setup and Procedures:
☐ Use grooved pin tuck foot, if you have one.
☐ Place feed dogs in normal up position.
☐ Guide presser foot or pin tucking foot along previously sewn stitching row to assure well spaced, even rows of pin tucking.

☐ Experiment with various sized needles and different feet.

The sashing on GOLDEN MEMORIES OF CHRISTMAS was quilted using a wide 4.0 mm double needle. The needle stitched through the fabric and batting created a "corded" appearance.

This fabric had printed diagonal lines which were followed for quilting eliminating the need to mark quilting lines.

Thready Loops

Long, silky loops of thread are made by winding a decorative thread around a 3″ x 5″ card. The loops

are then secured to the quilt by stitching over th center of the loops and then folding the loops in ha and stitching the base again. The loops themselve are then cut to avoid catching on other objects an tearing the quilt.

Heavy Threads and #5 Pearl Cotton

Thread that is too heavy to glide through th machine needle will work well in the bobbin. Th design is marked on the back and stitched from th back side. This gives a couched look to the surfac thread.

Thread ends should be secured by working int the batting. Allow several "loose inches" of threa at either end of heavy thread.

Special Fabrics

The use of an unusual fabric adds interest an surprise.

A washable metallic fabric completes the look an feel of the sunrise in TRANQUILITY.

Satin coat lining brings shine to the horns on this block from GOLDEN MEMORIES.

Ultra Suede

Ultra suede is washable, does not ravel and comes in a beautiful selection of color. It is also very expensive. A few scraps in a quilt are interesting as well as practical.

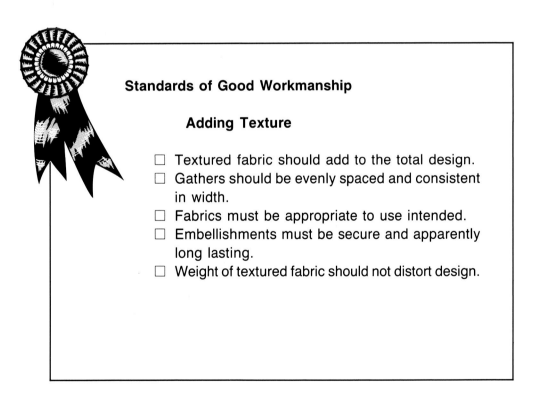

Standards of Good Workmanship

Adding Texture

☐ Textured fabric should add to the total design.
☐ Gathers should be evenly spaced and consistent in width.
☐ Fabrics must be appropriate to use intended.
☐ Embellishments must be secure and apparently long lasting.
☐ Weight of textured fabric should not distort design.

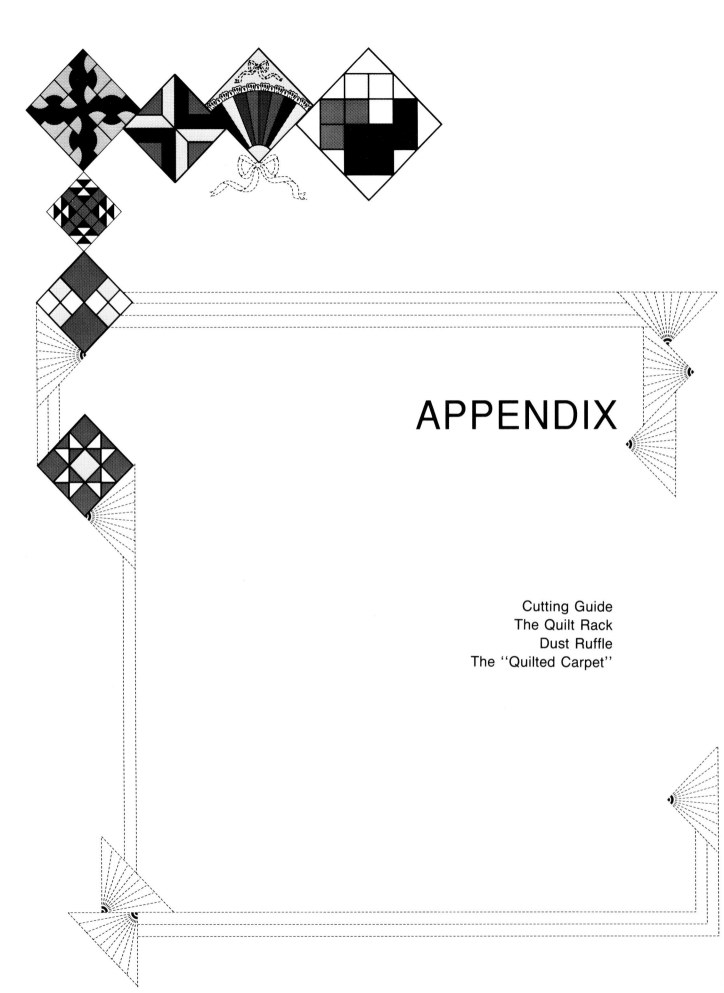

APPENDIX

Fabric Requirements

Cutting Layouts. Yardages are given for four different sizes of quilts. This should be an ample estimate of the yardage required for a SAMPLER quilt.

The sashing requires identical yardages for the front and back of the quilt. Use the same cutting diagram for either yardage. The layout is planned so that none of the long sashing strips will have to be pieced. If you do not mind an extra seam in the sashing, a smaller amount of fabric may be purchased.

If the sashing fabric that you have selected has a one way design, you may choose to cut the betweens and the top and bottom strips across the grain. Adequate yardage has been allowed but you will need to re-diagram the front cutting layout.

Fabric Requirement for Sampler Quilts
Based on 12" Blocks
4" Sashing

Bed Size	Crib	Twin	Double Queen	King
Mattress Size	23 x 46	39 x 75	54 x 75 60 x 80	76 x 80
Finished Quilt	33 x 48	68 x 84	88 x 104	104 x 104
# Blocks	6	20	20	25
Sashing	3"	4"	4"	4"
Additional Borders	None	None	10"	10"

Fabrics Required for Quilt Front

	Crib	Twin	Double Queen	King
Blocks (pieced) assorted	2 yds. assorted	7½ yds. assorted	7½ yds. assorted	8½ yds. assorted
Borders	None	None	3½ yds.	3½ yds.
Sashing	No additional requirement	4¼ yds.	4¼ yds.	5 yds.

Please Note: To find the fabric that best complements blocks, purchase *front sashing* fabric after blocks have been completed.

Fabric Required for Quilt Back

	Crib	Twin	Double Queen	King
Backing Totals	3¼ yds.	7½ yds.	11 yds.	12 yds.
Blocks	3¼ yds.	3¼ yds.	3¼ yds.	3½ yds.
Sashing	for both	4¼ yds.	4¼ yds.	5 yds.
Borders	None	None	3½ yds.	3½ yds.
Batting	Crib size	90 x 108	90 x 108	King size

Cutting Layout

Crib Size

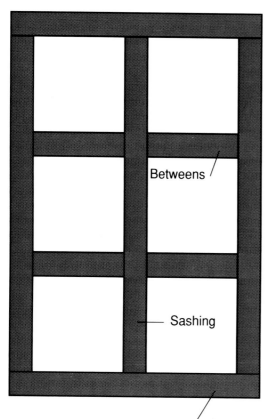

Betweens

Sashing

Perimeter Sashing

Crib Back & Front Sashing

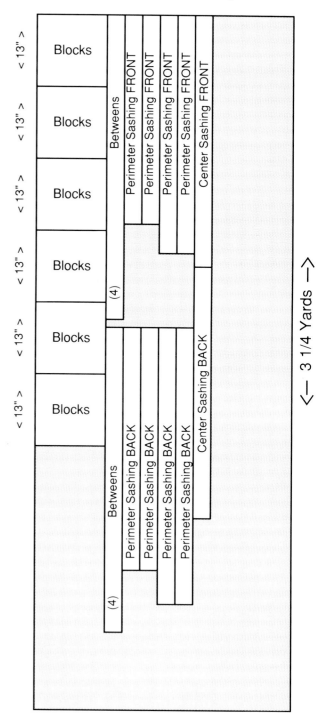

< 13" > Blocks
< 13" > Blocks
< 13" > Blocks
< 13" > Blocks
< 13" > Blocks
< 13" > Blocks

Betweens (4)

Perimeter Sashing FRONT
Perimeter Sashing FRONT
Perimeter Sashing FRONT
Perimeter Sashing FRONT
Center Sashing FRONT

Betweens (4)

Perimeter Sashing BACK
Perimeter Sashing BACK
Perimeter Sashing BACK
Perimeter Sashing BACK
Center Sashing BACK

<— 3 1/4 Yards —>

Mattress . . . . 23" x 46"

Finished quilt . . . . 33" x 48"

Blocks 6
    2 yards assorted fabrics

Sashing size . . . . 3"

Back Totals . . . . 3¼ yds.
    Includes *front sashing*

Batting . . . . Crib size

Cutting Layout

Twin Size

Mattress . . . . 39″ x 75″

Finished quilt . . . . 68″ x 84″

Blocks 20

Sashing Size . . . . 4″

Batting . . . . 90″ x 108″

Fabrics Required:

Blocks (front) . . . . 7½ yards

Sashing (front) . . . . 4¼ yards

Back Totals . . . . 7½ yards
   Blocks . . . . 3¼ yards
   Sashing . . . . 4¼ yards

Back Of Blocks

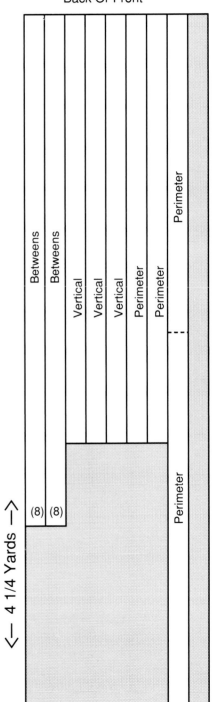

Sashing
Back Or Front

Cutting Layout

Double/Queen

Fabrics Required:

Mattress . . . . 54″ x 75″
                                       60″ x 80″

Finished quilt . . . . 88″ x 104″

Blocks 20

Sashing size . . . . 4″

Borders . . . . 10″

Blocks (front) . . . . 7½ yards

Sashing (front) . . . . 4¼ yards

Borders . . . . 3½ yards

Corner stones (optional) . . . . ½ yard

Back Totals . . . . 11 yards
    Blocks . . . . 3¼ yards
    Sashing . . . . 4¼ yards
    Borders . . . . 3½ yards

Batting . . . . 90″ x 108″

Back Of Blocks

< 13″ >	< 13″ >	< 15″ >
B	B	B
B	B	B
B	B	B
B	B	B
B	B	B
B	B	B
B	B	B
B	B	B
B	B	

← 3 1/4 Yards →

← 4 1/4 Yards →

Border Layout

← 3 1/2 Yards →

| 10″ | 10″ | 10″ | 10″ |

Sashing Back Or Front

Betweens · Betweens · Vertical · Vertical · Vertical · 2 Perimeter · 2 Perimeter · Perimeter

(8) (8)

Perimeter

Cutting Layout

King Size

Border Layout

<— 3 1/2 Yards —>

| 10" Border | 10" Border | 10" Border | 10" Border |

Mattress . . . . 76" x 80"

Finished quilt . . . . 104" x 104"

Blocks 25

Sashing . . . . 4"

Borders . . . . 10"

Fabrics Required:

Blocks (front) . . . . 8½ yards

Sashing (front) . . . . 5 yards

Borders . . . . 3½ yards

Corner Stones (optional) . . . . ½ yard

Back Totals . . . . 12 yards
    Blocks . . . . 3½ yards
    Sashing . . . . 5 yards
    Borders . . . . 3½ yards

Batting King Size . . . . . . 120" x 120"

Sashing
Back Or Front

<— 5 Yards —>

Betweens (10)
Betweens (10)
Vertical
Vertical
Vertical
Vertical
Perimeter
Perimeter
Perimeter
Perimeter

Back Of Blocks

< 13" > < 15" >

<— 3 1/2 Yards —>

B	B	B
B	B	B
B	B	B
B	B	B
B	B	B
B	B	B
B	B	B
B	B	B
B	B	B
B	B	B Extra

Lobstercage Quilt Rack

Not all quilts have to be on beds. Why not display a different quilt each season in your living area?

This charming quilt rack was made for my living room by a friend, Vernon Buppert. He said that he used five different types of wood in construction. It is stained to match the furniture in my living room and is tall enough to display a quilt well. It is a copy of an antique quilt rack found in New England.

One of the beauties of this quilt rack is the sweeping curve of the "cage" which shows a quilt to its best advantage while protecting the fabrics of the quilt from stress or strain.

Specifications:

Pieces:

Item	Qty.	Description	Dimensions
(A)	2	vertical supports	3½″ x 1½″ x 40″
(B)	2	dowel support	1″ diameter x 40″
(C)	2	base	5¼″ x 1½″ x 20″
(D)	1	horizontal support	4½″ x 1½″ x 36″
(E)	10	dowels	1″ diameter x 36″

**Note that the vertical support height can be altered to accommodate a larger quilt.

Quilt Rack specs by Ed Smith

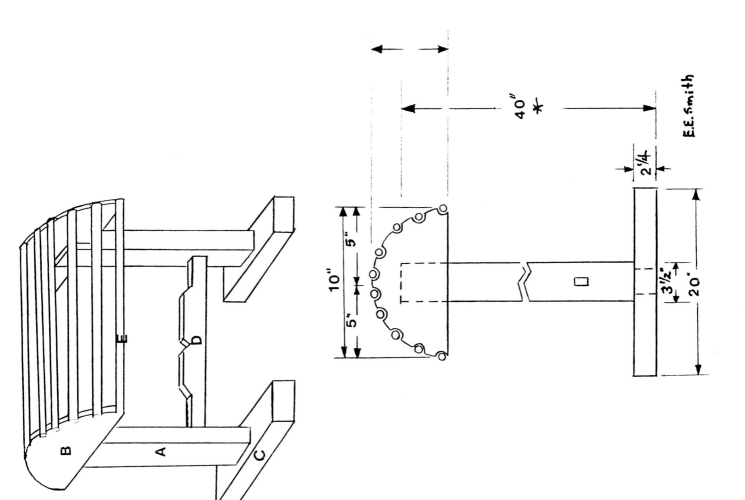

E.E.Smith

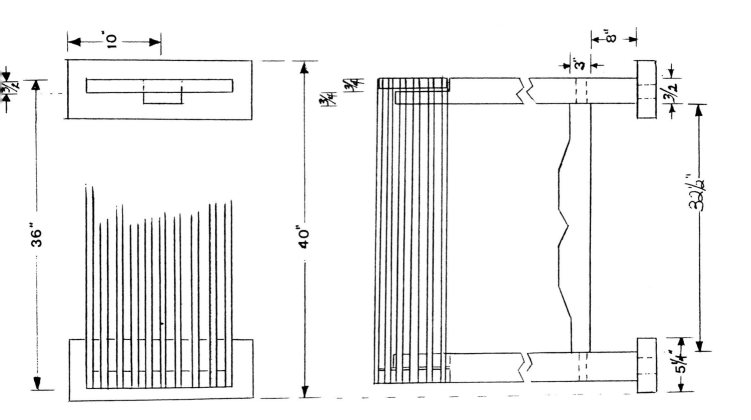

Dust Ruffle

A dust ruffle completes the quilt ensemble. Sewn to a foundation the size of the mattress and placed between the mattress and box spring, the dust ruffle stays in place and hangs evenly.

The ruffle, made in three pieces, can be used with or without a bed footboard. The dust ruffle will overlap slightly at the corners giving a "one piece" look. If a one piece ruffle is desired, sew fabric sections together and distribute fullness evenly.

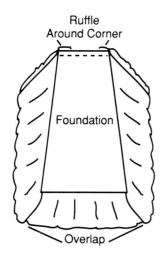

Ruffle Around Corner

Foundation

Overlap

Yardage:

Ruffles:
Twin Size: 4¼ yds., Double: 5¾ yds., Queen/King: 6½ yds.

Foundation: fitted sheet or muslin
Twin: 2¼ yds., Double: 4¼ yds., Queen/King: 4½ yds.

Notions: Elastic thread

Foundation will be sandwiched between the mattress and the box springs:
☐ Seam muslin and cut into mattress size plus seam allowances or use fitted sheet.
☐ Hem upper edge near headboard.

Ruffles:
☐ Determine depth:
  • Measure distance from top of box spring to floor.
  • Add ¼ " for top seam allowance and 1½" for bottom hem.
☐ Determine length of fabric needed for ruffles:
  • Double length of sides plus 5" for seaming and overlap.
  • Double mattress width plus 2½" for hems.
☐ Hem: Press and stitch a 1" hem on long and two short sides of each piece.
☐ Gather Unhemmed Edges:
  • With elastic thread in the bobbin, run a row of straight stitches ¼ " from raw edge. Fabric will automatically gather.
    To increase gathering:
      • lengthen stitch
      • tighten tension of upper thread
  • Alternate gathering methods:
      • Use machine ruffler or gathering foot
      • Stitch two parallel rows, 6 stitches/inch. Pull bobbin thread to gather.

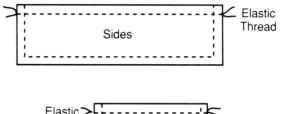

Sides

Elastic Thread

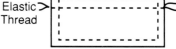

Elastic Thread

☐ Attach ruffles to foundation:
  • Distribute gathers evenly.
  • Attach ruffles to three unhemmed edges of foundation with ¼ " seam allowance.
  • Extend ruffles around corners at headboard end.
  • Overlap gathered corners at foot about 2".
  • Over cast or serge raw edges to eliminate raveling.

The Quilted Carpet

Your home will say, "A quiltmaker lives here!" when the carpet itself is a medallion quilt in colors that match and enhance your decor. High quality remnants can be purchased to create a unique and beautiful floor covering which is relatively inexpensive and very easy to do.

A no-sew quilt block rug can be made in a day with a pattern, rug knife, carpet cement and a roll or two of single faced carpet tape. Several yards of sturdy burlap are also required.

Color and texture are important in making a successful rug. Shades and tints of a given color add a subtle interest. High and low piles, twists and loops all combine to create an interesting surface.

Figure how much carpet is required by measuring your room. Then scout around for interesting textures and colors that blend together to enhance your furnishings. Often the carpet store will cut a large remnant into strips for the borders. That is a big help!

The rug will be a simple MEDALLION quilt on the floor. It will have a pieced center which will be set into a larger piece of carpet and framed by borders. The block center will be glued to burlap with carpet cement (purchased by the gallon at the hardware store.)

The borders that frame the center square will be secured with single faced carpet tape which is very strong and durable. The outside edge of the carpet will be bound in carpet tape that you will be able to purchase at the carpet remnant shop.

Directions For Quilt Block Rug

☐ Select a favorite quilt block pattern. The Ohio Star or Rolling Stone works well. Almost any fairly simple design will be easy to fabricate in carpet. There is no problem piecing into the corner as everything will be glued not sewn.

☐ Enlarge a 12″ block pattern by a factor of three. A 12″ block will create a rug center that is 3 feet square. Make templates for the pattern pieces out of poster board. There is no seam allowance to be added. Grainline is very important, however. The carpet will shade due to the nap or pile.

☐ Seam burlap, if necessary, to create one piece of fabric large enough to back medallion area.

☐ Draw block design on burlap using templates and marking pen.

☐ Draw and cut carpet pieces using templates and carpet knife. Work from the back side of the carpet. A metal yardstick can act as a cutting guide.

☐ Position cut carpet pieces on burlap design to verify color placement and exact fit of pieces.

☐ Remove design. Spread carpet cement on burlap and reposition carpet design pieces. (Work on a sheet of plastic as glue may soak through burlap.)

☐ Trim burlap to exact size of medallion.

☐ Determine "insert position" of medallion in larger carpet.
  • Use templates to recreate design area on back of carpet.
  • Check for accuracy.
  • Cut out the center of the carpet.
  • Replace "cutout area" with medallion.
  • Secure with single faced carpet tape.

Note: The carpet pieces fit together snuggly looking like a one piece carpet. I have never had a problem with little pieces of carpet pulling away from backing.

☐ Borders can enlarge the rug to any desired size. Have them cut for you at your carpet shop, if possible. Be especially careful of the nap and grainline when you position them on rug. Use single faced tape to secure.

☐ Bind the floor quilt with a purchased rug binding.
  • Place binding on rug, rights sides together.
  • Staple carpet tape to carpet edge:
    • staple ⅜ to ½″ from edge of carpet
    • run a continuous row of staples.

☐ Turn binding to back and glue in place with carpet cement.

Now you have a quilt that doesn't have to be treated with "white gloves."

A basement floor can be "quilted" for practically nothing. Collect carpet scraps from your friends and the carpet shop. Sort them by color. Apply carpet glue directly to the clean cement. Work the pattern in an organized "crazy quilt" fashion. A quilted basement floor is really fun and inexpensive.

OHIO STAR

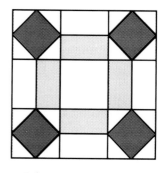

ROLLING STONE

Photo Credit Index

Bibliography

Beyer, Jinny; *Patchwork Patterns*, EPM Publications, Inc., McLean, VA, 1979.

Beyer, Jinny; *The Quilter's Album of Blocks & Borders*, EPM Publications, Inc., McLean, VA, 1980.

Colby, Averil; *Quilting*, Charles Scribner's Sons, New York, 1971.

Dodson, Jackie; *Know Your Bernina*, Chilton Book Company, Radnor, PA, 1987.

Ericson, Lois; *Fabrics . . . Reconstructed*, (Lois Ericson, Box 1680, Tahoe City, CA, 95730), 1986.

Ericson, Lois; *Texture . . . A Closer Look*, Eric's Press, Box 1680, Tahoe City, CA, 95730, 1987.

Hazen, Gale; *Sew Sane*, Cambrian News, San Jose, CA, 1985.

Myers, Jan; *Dyeing*, Jan Myers, 7422 Ben Hur St. Pittsburg, PA, 15208.

Millard, Debra; *A Quilter's Guide To Fabric Dyeing*, 7500 South Ulster Place, Englewood, CO 80112, 1984.

Sources of Supplies

Books

American Quilter's Society
P.O. Box 3290
Paducah, KY 42002-3290
(1-800)626-5420

Dover St. Booksellers
P.O. Box 1563
39 E. Dover St.
Easton, MD 21601
(301)822-9329

Fabric Dyeing

Cerulean Blue, Ltd.
P.O. Box 21168
Seattle, WA 98111-3168
(206)443-7744
Catalog: $5.00

Pro Chemical & Dye
P.O. Box 14
Somerset, MA 027226
(617)676-3838

Testfabrics, Inc.
P.O. Drawer "O"
Middlesex, NJ 808846
(201)469-6446

Mail Order Fabrics

G Street Fabrics
11854 Rockville Pike
Rockville, MD 20853
(301)231-8998

Seminole Sampler
71 Mellor Road
Catonsville, MD 21228
(301)788-1720

Notions

Aardvark Adventures
P.O. Box 2449
Livermore, CA 94550

Clotile, Inc.
237 SW 28th Street
Ft. Lauderdale, FL 33315
(305)761-8655

Sew Art International
(invisible thread)
P.O. Box 550
Bountiful, UT 84010
(1-800)231-2787

Coffey Creations
(Quilt Pattern Organizer
Quilt Pattern Pocket Sheets)
P.O. Box 124
Green Spring, WV 26722
(304)492-5907

Speed Stitch
3113 Broadpoint Drive
Harbor Heights, FL 33983
Catalogue $3.00 (refundable)

Pictures In Quilts

The Emporium Outlet
Sharp CX 5000
431 Dual Hwy. – Venice Inn
Hagerstown, MD 21740

Classie Calicoes
(Iron-on film for
photo transfer)
4821 Bel Pre Road
Rockville, MD 20853
(301)460-5648